†From *JOHN WAYNE: American* by Randy Roberts and James S. Olson. Copyright © 1995 by James S. Olson and Randy Roberts. Reprinted with permission of The Free Press, a Division of Simon & Schuster.

FIRST EDITION

Designer: G. H. DeLong, Jr., DeLong and Company, Gainesville, Georgia.
Printed by Matthews Printing Company, Gainesville, Georgia.
Bindery: Rand McNally Book Services, Nashville, Tennessee.

ISBN 0-9655107-0-0

The Featherbone Principle

A DECLARATION OF INTERDEPENDENCE

Charles E. "Gus" Whalen, Jr.

with
PHILLIP ROB BELLURY

Foreword by
PHILIP M. CONDIT
President and CEO, The Boeing Company

Foreword

By Philip M. Condit

*H*ardly anything else comes into the world as helpless as a human baby. We just can't cut it without a lot of support. As we grow up, we try at every opportunity to exercise our independence from the very people who helped us from the beginning, testing the patience of our parents, friends and teachers. And we are encouraged at times to try our own wings.

There are little milestones along the way — being trusted to walk alone to the store, leaving mom and dad to attend school, and the really big symbol of freedom in our teen years, taking the family car out for a solo spin. Finishing our education and finding a job cuts us loose even more, and many of us resist the commitment of marriage for a while because we are enjoying our "independence" so much.

Then we spend another half a lifetime coming to the realization that we never were, never will be and never can be completely on our own. In our older years, we actually gain a lot of comfort in knowing there are people we can rely on to help us on our way.

The earlier in life that a person or a company realizes the truth of — and the power of — interdependence, the more successful they become.

The Boeing Company advertising tag that we used for a time, "No One Flies Alone", was in recognition of the fact that when you fly in one of our products, there are thousands of people all around the world working together who make it possible.

Interdependence, as the word indicates, is a two-way deal. We can't expect to get a lot of help from others unless we understand the responsibility we each have to do our part.

Gus Whalen captures the essence of this truth in *The Featherbone Principle: A Declaration of Interdependence.*

Phil Condit
President & CEO
The Boeing Company

*This book is dedicated to my father, Charles E. Whalen, Sr.,
who taught me to BE, and to my stepmother, Doris A. Whalen,
who taught me to DO.*

We need both.

Reflections On The Western Hero

John Wayne was the embodiment of the Western hero. Rock solid. Impenetrable. An uncommon confidence. And, most of all, a fierce independence. A man who faced unbelievable peril with no need or desire for help from anyone. In most of his movies, John Wayne's rough and tumble cowboys set out to do it alone and never seemed to fail at getting the job done.

In their book, *John Wayne: American*, his biographers wrote: "Western heroes tended to be unattached, independent men, free from family responsibilities, free even from the encumbrances of friends and neighbors. They appear suddenly out of the vast landscapes and disappear back into them. Only unattached men are capable of the violence required out West; families and communities come with strings attached, knotted by law, culture and civilization."†

This book tries to answer a few questions: In reality, in our businesses and personal lives, can the independent hero, acting alone and motivated by a desire to eliminate the competition, better his position or get revenge, really get the job done? Or is there a better way? After some serious *"rethinking"*, I believe there is a better way. I hope as you read this book, you will too.

FOREWORD

FOR THE HEROES
ACKNOWLEDGMENTS
ABOUT THE AUTHOR

E. K. Warren

CHAPTER ONE

A Featherbrained Idea

"In its own quiet way, (Warren Featherbone Company) is a reminder that, even in this restive financial era, there is a core to U. S. business that has value and tradition, and that endures."

Excerpt from THE WALL STREET JOURNAL, May 1989,

written by Eric Morgenthaler

*I*n 1882, my great-grandfather, Edward Kirk Warren, took a feather from a turkey and conceived an idea that would revolutionize an industry. It was a simple idea, but no less ingenious than the invention of the automobile; and in the world of ladies fashion, no less important.

From his idea a remarkable new product was spawned. A

thriving company followed. Now, well over a century later, it safely can be said that thousands of lives were affected in countless ways, and almost always for the better. Consciously or unconsciously, my great-grandfather unlocked the door to success and entered in. There is much that can be learned from his story and the company he founded.

E. K. Warren began his career at the age of sixteen as a clerk in a dry-goods store. He worked 12 to 14 hours a day, slept on the counter at night and for his efforts received a mere 50 cents a day. It was pure drudgery for little reward, but he persevered. Several years later, he became a partner in the store and eventually purchased the business.

While he was still a storekeeper, E. K. recognized a need in the womens dress industry for a cheaper and more pliable stay material to replace whalebone. Whalebone was very expensive. Over time, it would become brittle and crack. And it was common knowledge that large-scale whaling operations were taking their toll on the whale population. In fact, whales were fast becoming extinct.

During a visit to a feather duster manufacturing plant, E. K.

MAKING FEATHERBONE

Circular shears cut the plumage from the turkey feather. The plumage was used for stuffing mattresses.

The quills were then split in half, exposing the pith.

The pith was removed by a pair of rollers sheathed in sandpaper. Rich in nitrogen, the pith was sold as fertilizer.

Another set of cutters divided the half-quill into a series of narrow strips about 8" long.

Scores of young women fed bundles of quill strips into machines which bound them with thread to form single strands.

Four strands were then fed into a machine which bound them together into a flat strip of Featherbone.

observed that turkey quills by the thousands were regularly discarded. He saw piles and piles of what feather duster manufacturers referred to as "bones of contention." E. K. pondered the large quantities of "despised pointer quills" and wondered if he was witnessing a missed opportunity. A closer examination of

the quills proved him right. The pliable physical properties of the turkey quill, if properly processed, could provide a superior, low-cost substitute for whalebone.

After considerable toil and experimentation, my great-grandfather coined

We're not sure, but we suspect that Budweiser saw this early 1900 Featherbone magazine ad.

the term "featherbone" and introduced it to the market in 1883. Entirely new manufacturing processes were developed and special machinery was patented and built for transforming the quills into featherbone. He believed in producing a quality product and worked hard to perfect a boning material that was acceptable to dressmakers, merchants and consumers.

His efforts paid off. By the turn of the century, Warren's featherbone was the preferred choice of wholesale and retail drygoods merchants across the country. In 1901, the famous actress Sarah Bernhardt commented that Warren's featherbone was the best dress boning material in existence and was always used in her costumes. That same year, an article from the company's widely distributed "Featherbone Magazinette" described featherbone's emergence this way: *"The ingenuity of the inventor, the painstaking care of the manufacturers, the satisfaction of the merchant, the skill of the dressmaker and the comfort of the lady who wears it, give full explanation of the success of Warren's Featherbone."*

Featherbone was here to stay. The word "featherbone" became a generic term and made its way into the dictionary. That the word immediately precedes "featherbrain" was probably not lost on my great-grandfather; he was, after all, an observant man. Hopefully, he also possessed a good sense of humor.

feath•er•bed•ding (feth' er bed' ing), *n.* a type of coercion of an employer by a labor union, in which the employer is forced to pay for services not performed, esp. by hiring unnecessary employees.
feath•er•bone (feth' er bon'), *n.* a substitute for whalebone, made from the quills of domestic fowls.
feath•er•brain (feth' er bran'), *n.* a giddy or weak-minded person. **—feth'er•brained'**, *adj.*

THE FABRIC OF A COMMUNITY

The Warren Featherbone Company began operations in the tiny village of Three Oaks, Michigan, near the shores of Lake Michigan in the extreme southwest corner of the state. E. K. was 36 years old when he capitalized the company in October of 1883. Within a few months, his plant was running full tilt with a crew of nine. A decade later, his employees numbered in the hundreds.

As the company grew, so grew the village. By the turn of

THREE OAKS, MICHIGAN 1906

the century, the population of Three Oaks more than doubled. The welfare of the village became inextricably tied to the success of the company. The leaders of the community understood this all too well and once issued a letter to the Warren Featherbone Company urging Mr. Warren to ignore any thoughts of pulling up stakes and leaving.

For his part, E. K. remained faithful to the community, refusing tempting offers to sell or move in order to maintain the prosperity of the area. A local newspaper at the time ran an article describing his commitment to furnishing "profitable employment to the children of those who were his former school-mates."

E. K. Warren possessed an uncommon sense of community. He used his influence and money to secure a railroad stop and depot at Three Oaks. He worked for better roads. He was instrumental in giving the town a municipal water and lighting plant. And, convinced that the liquor traffic was a demoralizing influence, he fought forcefully against saloons and the selling of liquor.

He believed in Three Oaks, and did all he could do to enrich the lives of the people there. If a spirit of unity and pride was woven into the fabric of life in Three Oaks, then E. K. Warren was the weaver. Perhaps no other event exemplifies this better than the remarkable story of the Dewey Cannon.

In 1899, the U.S. government authorized a national committee to raise funds for a war memorial. The result was a nationwide contest to see which city or town could make the largest per capita contribution. The prize was an ancient brass cannon, of Spanish origin, which had been taken from the Corregidor Island in Manila Bay by Admiral George Dewey.

For E. K. Warren, the challenge was irresistible. He called a mass meeting of the town's citizens and proposed that Three Oaks enter the race. A slogan, "Three Oaks Against The World" was adopted, and over time the tiny village received national publicity for its audacity to take on the world. The citizens, of course, responded enthusiastically to the challenge and, with a per capita subscription of $1.41, won the prize.

The victory drew even more national attention to Three Oaks. Dewey Park was developed in the center of town as a permanent site for the cannon, and plans were laid for the unveiling the next summer. But before that event occurred, the town was visited by none other than U. S. President William McKinley. The event of his coming, and the subsequent unveiling, were both attended by thousands.

Winning the Dewey Cannon was a much-heralded victory for the community of Three Oaks, and one that raised their sense of togetherness to an all-time high. Through his leadership in such events, E. K. Warren had erased most of the distance that often exists between business and the community. In Three Oaks, the two were clearly *interdependent*.

A MAN WITH A MISSION . . .

Beyond his sense of community, there was another dimension to my great-grandfather's life. It was well-known that he was visionary and a man with broad purpose. Two areas of interest in his life attest to his extraordinary world view.

First was his leadership in the World Sunday School movement. He poured an abundance of time and resources into its evolution. In 1904, he carried through the immense project of holding the Fourth International Sunday School Convention in Jerusalem, and he personally chartered an ocean liner so that 800 U.S. delegates could attend the gathering. A few years later, he conceived and helped to organize, as part of the Sunday School Convention, a Samaritan committee, whose purpose was to provide education and financial support to the people of Samaria. It was his long-cherished purpose to show the spirit of the good Samaritan to surviving Samaritans. An interesting and worthy concept, it resulted in a flood of practical support for the welfare of that country.

E. K.'s untiring efforts as a churchman were the result of his strong belief in a progressive gospel. To him, the Acts of the Apostles was a great unfinished work in which every true disciple was writing his chapter. He wanted to write a chapter of his own, and he vigorously did.

The other example of E. K.'s vision and purpose had to do with one of his largest assets — land. Long before it was popular, he became a conservationist. His most precious conservation project was a 320-acre tract of timberland just north of Three Oaks. "Warren's Woods" was originally purchased for the purpose of manufacturing charcoal from the timber, but that venture proved unsuccessful. In the meantime, however, E. K. came to appreciate the great beauty of virgin hardwood timber. As a result, he not only ceased the charcoal operation, but also the tapping of the maple trees there. Today, Warren Woods State Park is one of the few remaining, intact examples of climax beech-maple forests that once covered the upper Midwest.

The rapid industrial development of areas outside the Chicago area heightened his concern for the future of forest land. Likewise, he was concerned that as these natural resources gave way to progress, the heritage of the region would be lost for future generations. Over time this concern led to the establishment of the Chamberlain Memorial Museum and later, the Edward K. Warren Foundation. The museum and the Warren Woods wildlife preserve were brought under this umbrella organization.

Another tract along the shores of Lake Michigan was preserved as well, and later donated to the state. Today, Warren Dunes State Park contains 1900 acres, with $2^1/_2$ miles of Lake Michigan shoreline. With more than one million visitors annually, it is one of the most highly-visited state parks in Michigan, providing both a recreational haven and an undeveloped natural sand dune habitat.

By the time of his death in 1919, E. K. Warren's contributions to his family, community, church and industry were already legendary. Through the Foundation, he dispersed the bulk of his accumulated wealth — over seven million dollars — to philanthropic causes. In today's economy, that amount would be valued at more than $63 million, not including the appreciated value of his real estate contribution.

E. K.'s passing probably left an emotional void in the hearts of many people in the company and in the community. But the literal and figurative foundation that he left behind more than filled that void. He established a sense of family in both his business and his community that lasted for generations, and he advanced his personal causes far beyond anyone's wildest expectations.

CRISIS, CRISIS, CRISIS!

In 1920, my grandfather, Frederick Chamberlain, succeeded to the presidency of the Warren Featherbone Company. Under his leadership, the company expanded into the notions market. Sewing notions were especially popular during the turn of the century and included small, useful items such as blanket binding, tie cords, girdles, boned belting and garters, all of which were manufactured by Warren Featherbone. One item, a new and revolutionary bias tape, possessed a softness and color range that rocked competitors on their feet.

But during the thirties, the changing women's fashion scene reduced the market for notions and featherbone dramatically. The company's mainstay, the featherbone, found new, formidable competition in the form of *plastic*. Plastic offered two significant challenges to the viability of featherbone: One, it was a better material and, two, it was cheaper. Try to compete against that!

Faced with its first major crisis, the company realized that if it were to survive, new markets and products would have to be developed. Working with B. F. Goodrich in Akron, Ohio, the company developed a number of new consumer items, including garment bags, children's rainwear, and bibs — all made from a vinyl resin film (plastic) called Koroseal. Then someone (no one is sure who) in the company formed a piece of plastic into what proved to be the best product since the featherbone itself — *plastic waterproof baby pants.*

This new product served as a welcome replacement for the hot and sweaty latex rubber pants because they were — you guessed it — cheaper and better. Like its founder fifty years earlier, the company created a winner from a pile of scraps. More than any other product, plastic baby pants put The Warren Featherbone Company back on the road to prosperity, and maybe more importantly for the future, launched the company's entry into the childrens apparel market. *Plastic, the adversary, had become the company's best friend.*

This renewed prosperity was interrupted in the early forties by World War II. To help with the war effort, the company redirected its manufacturing operations toward wartime products. Many of the men left to fight overseas; women in Three Oaks went to work in the factory.

By this time, H. H. Cutler had succeeded Frederick Chamberlain as president of the company. In the company's lengthy history, he was to be the only non-family president, leading the company through the critical war years and into the next decade. Cutler left Warren Featherbone to start his own successful infantswear manufacturing company, which today is a division of VF Corporation.

In business, as in all other areas of life, change is inevitable. By the early fifties, the Warren Featherbone Company was completely out of the notions business. The competition for its primary product, plastic baby pants, was fierce. It had expanded its clothing operations by purchasing two Atlanta-based manufacturers of infantswear, Alexis, Inc., and Handi-Panti, Inc. Other companies, including Warren Featherbone's suppliers, were moving south for better conditions and climate.

Charles E. Whalen, my father, became president of the company in 1949. He had just lost his wife (and my mother) to polio. (My mother was the granddaughter of E. K. Warren.) The company was struggling financially. The plant was old and operations were increasingly outdated. It was time for a change.

My father was in a crisis situation, faced with a radically difficult decision. After almost three-quarters of a century of faithful partnership with the community of Three Oaks, how could the company pull up stakes and leave? What would happen to the community that had depended so much on Warren Featherbone for its survival?

Emotionally, the decision must have been especially difficult. He was leaving generations of family and friends. From a business perspective, it may have been much less difficult. Something had to be done. As for the impact on the community, the truth was that jobs were anything but scarce. The rapid industrialization of southern Michigan and Chicago's urban sprawl created an abundance of employment opportunities in the area. All things considered, there was every reason to make a move.

Even so, my father enabled the company's purchasing agent, Oscar Knoll, to set up his own company in Three Oaks to preserve local jobs. Warren Featherbone provided patterns and start-up technology to help this new company establish itself. This company later became the Knoll Division of Gerber Baby Foods and the largest producer of baby pants in the United States, if not the world. Ironically, in a few short years, they became Warren Featherbone's chief competitor for that product.

So the company moved. For a brief period during the mid-fifties, the company continued operations in Three Oaks as well as their new location, Gainesville, Georgia. By 1958, however, all operations in Three Oaks ceased, and the Warren Featherbone Company became a Georgia-based manufacturer.

If the citizens of Three Oaks mourned the company's departure, it was little compared to the welcome it received in Gainesville. The small north Georgia community received the company with open arms. In a letter written by my father in 1957, he described his new environment: "Gainesville is located about 35 miles northeast of Atlanta, in the foothills of the Blue Ridge Mountains. The climate here is much milder than in Michigan. The people of Gainesville, through the Chamber of Commerce, put out a bond issue to finance the construction of the plant, which is just being completed."

With the move came many adjustments, of course, and the financial struggles did not disappear. But the company held together and headed into the sixties with a commitment to become as successfully integrated into the economy of Gainesville as it had been in Three Oaks. The apparel industry was growing, and Warren Featherbone wanted to grow with it.

Ultimately, my father's decision to move the company proved to be the right one. Unfortunately, he died before he could really see the best results of that decision. At the time of his death in 1969, the company was still struggling to find its niche in the industry. Throughout the fifties and sixties, the company had concentrated its efforts on marketing plastic products for children. But another crisis was looming, and this time the burden for dealing with it fell on inexperienced and untested shoulders.

I came to work at the Warren Featherbone Company in 1967. What attracted me to the company was its heritage and its values that had proved effective over time. In spite of its difficulties in the marketplace, I felt the company had a lot going for it. But I was still in my early twenties, and the idea of succeeding my father was the farthest thing from my mind.

His untimely death got my attention in a hurry. My stepmother, Doris, and I assumed responsibility for the future of the company. She had worked in the company as an artist and designer, and I had limited experience in sales. We were joined by Evelyn Dunagan, the company's comptroller and director. The three of us comprised the leadership team. Ultimately, Doris would prove to be one of the great creative talents in our company's history. As Chief Financial Officer, Evelyn's contributions in many areas have been immeasurable.

Our greatest assets as newfound leaders were twofold: one, we knew we didn't have all the answers, and two, we were surrounded by people in the company who did. In the years following, we leaned heavily on our greatest resource, the people in the company, and they came through in a big way.

In the late sixties and early seventies another shift in the diaper industry created yet another significant crisis for the Warren Featherbone Company. Our plastic baby pants met the most formidable competitor of all: *disposable diapers*. As Americans flocked to supermarkets to purchase *Pampers*®, use of cloth diapers — and plastic covers — saw a dramatic decline. Plastic pants still accounted for the bulk of the company's sales, and once again, we faced a tremendous challenge to our survival.

For solutions we looked to our past, and the message was clear. We had to adapt. So we refashioned our line of infantswear and concentrated our marketing and merchandising efforts toward the high-quality department store. We revamped our sales and marketing staff, creating four national sales regions to better service the department store market. And finally, we developed an item called "diaper dress-ups," which were fancy coverings worn *over* disposable diapers.

All these adaptive moves paid off. Today, the company turns out about 7 million pieces of infantswear a year, mostly under the *Alexis*™ label. We have approximately 2,600 commercial customers, including most of the large department store chains in the United States. We have entered international markets in Canada, Europe and Japan. We have significantly increased our domestic production in a period when U. S.-based manufacturing has declined. And, yes, we still sell those diaper dress-ups, which account for about 5 percent of Warren Featherbone sales.

As we approach the end of the century, and our company continues to grow, we still look to our past for better understanding of what lies ahead. As we have done that, we've learned a lot about the importance of being connected within our organization, with the communities where we conduct business, and with others in our industry. We have a deeper understanding of our broader mission; we're not just another apparel company, but part of a larger whole. We have a role to play in that larger whole, which is limited only by how much energy we are willing to commit to it. Finally, we know that crisis is inevitable. We know it's on the way, and like a freight train just around the bend, we see the reflection of its headlights and hear the wail of its horn as it draws near. But believe it or not, we're not afraid. We think the train is bringing us something we can use. *We plan to get on board.*

To some degree, the principles we've learned from our past are what this book is all about. But our recent history has taught us even more. Some of the stories you will read in subsequent chapters may seem miraculous. Some may remind you of your own situation. Some are still unfolding. But in all of them, there are important messages. Principles that work. Lessons to be learned. Promise for the future.

12/22/92

Mr. Whalen,

Years ago when I worked for your Company, I took a pair of pants and a cap. It has bothered me ever since, I'm asking for forgiveness. I enclose $5 for restitution. I'm witholding my name to protect my family. Please Accept my apology.

CHAPTER TWO

Still Family After All These Years

Dear Mr. Whalen:

Years ago, when I worked for your company, I took a pair of pants and a cap. It has bothered me ever since. I'm asking for forgiveness. I enclose $5 for restitution. I'm withholding my name to protect my family. Please accept my apology.

few years ago, three days before Christmas, I received this letter in the mail. I was intrigued by its content and wondered what to make of it. What motivated the writer to seek forgiveness and make restitution? Did that motivation have anything to do with how we conduct business at Warren Featherbone? For help in answering these questions, I sought the advice of our company's *"Rethink Group."*

The Rethink Group was established in 1991 as part of a larger cross-functional effort within our industry. Several companies each formed Rethink teams, which came together to address specific issues related to the way we operate as a supply system. Our own Rethink Group's function within the company has a similar purpose, but focuses on what people at Warren Featherbone do and can do to make the company a better place to work. Over time, this group has been an invaluable source of ideas and solutions.

I made copies of the "Christmas Letter", as it came to be known, and circulated it among the Rethink team members. Everyone was asked to think about the letter over the holidays and return to the group with their reflections. Their written responses were insightful, relevant and sincere. They all emphasized the importance of *integrity, values,* and *forgiveness.* One in particular seemed to sum up nearly everyone's thoughts. But more than that, it led us to a new and more precise understanding of who we are as a company. That response from one individual was a simple, but profound, statement: *"Still family after all these years."*

The Family Business

Frankly, family-owned businesses typically do not have good track records. Only about a third of all family-owned businesses survive beyond the first generation, and fewer than 15 percent become third-generation companies. Why? There are many contributing factors, of course, but one reason has to do with the history of family businesses in general.

The family business is an extension of the family farm concept. Historically, the farm was organized and run by the family for the sole purpose of supporting the family. On a farm that concept might work, but for a business to survive over a long period of time, it's not enough.

The nuclear family in a family-owned business often becomes a major threat to the company's success. The trouble begins *when they can't see a purpose beyond protecting the welfare of the family.* As a result, they feel disconnected from others in the company. There's *"we"* and *"they"*. The family can even become factional and isolated, leading to a downward spiral in their relationships within the family and within the company. Unless a vision is passed on by the founders, the dream for the business can become a nightmare for all those who inherit it.

Any traditional family business has a greater chance of long-term survival when there is a vision greater than the business itself. A broader purpose. A sense of mission that is passed from one generation to the next. And members of the core family have to discover connections that exist between people inside *and* outside the company, and outside their industry. As in any organization, there has to be a movement from *we-they* to *us*.

BUILDING BLOCKS
1. **Creative thinking**
2. **Find a need and fill it**
3. **Value oriented**
4. **People oriented**
5. **Hard work**
6. **Enthusiasm**
7. **Ability to adapt**

How do we do this? First, we ask ourselves these meaningful questions: What business are we in? What is our role in this business, and where does this business fit in a much larger context? We have to get *outside* of where we are. If we're only looking for meaning in our lives inside our own organizational walls, we won't find it.

Any organization has a belief system. In our case, it started from day one with E. K. Warren. He put his beliefs into practice, and they have lasted through the years. Over time, people in the company have chosen different ways of manifesting those beliefs, but still they remain. Based on the Judeo-Christian ethic, they certainly weren't our invention, but they are rock-solid building blocks: *honesty, faith,* and *hard work.*

Somehow that ethic has survived, handed down from generation to generation, and today the culture of the company is pretty much the same as it was over a hundred years ago. We still use those building blocks to grow the company, and I'm convinced that what will keep us — or any company — going is maintaining a strong ethic. In companies where it doesn't exist, or it isn't clearly understood, the chances of survival diminish.

The "Christmas Letter" story is an encouraging indication that the writer, in his or her experience with our company, saw honesty in practice. The letter probably would never have been written had the culture been otherwise. We mirror what we're around. The writer responded to the mistake by asking forgiveness and seeking restitution. He or she was part of the Warren Featherbone family while working here and felt that a connection had been broken. It must have been difficult to write the letter, but apparently the desire to stay connected with others in this company was strong enough to warrant it. *Still family after all these years.*

Twenty years ago, someone in our company acted on a bright idea and changed forever the way we celebrate Christmas inside our facilities. She asked her supervisor if she could decorate her sewing machine. The idea took root and flourished. Others followed her lead. Today, all the sewing machines are decorated during the Christmas season. I doubt there's a mall in America with more decorations per square inch than we have at Warren Featherbone. And, it's all volunteer.

Christmas is an especially wonderful time to lead visitors on a tour of our facility in Gainesville. People often compliment us on our cleanliness and seem to be impressed by the care we give to our working environment. But the view across the plant of all those bright decorations leads to even higher praise. It can be downright inspiring.

The joy of Christmas inside our plant has been elevated to a new level by the actions of one person twenty years ago. It wouldn't have happened in an environment where it wasn't supported philosophically. It wasn't just a matter of giving permission; it was instead an enthusiastic endorsement of a good idea. There may be sterile environments where people would love to decorate for Christmas, but the culture doesn't support it.

Reflections on Christmas at Warren Featherbone
by James E. Mathis, Sr.
Retired Chairman of the Board, Trust Company Bank of North Georgia.

A few days before Christmas a year or two ago, Gus invited me for a plant tour. I had heard of the Christmas decorations in the sewing room, but little did I expect what I found. Nor did my brain assemble what was happening there at that time. I came to find out the employees <u>wanted</u> to decorate for Christmas — each machine operator had designed and decorated the air space around and within their own work areas. The sewing room is one large open area. The sewing machines are in rows, and the conduits hang from the ceiling above supplying energy to each operator's equipment. Hanging down and around was roping, tinsel, Christmas ornaments, a variety of decorations — each area different. I first thought, "What a mess." But then, like a dimensional painting with hidden faces, the decorations began *to take on form, depth, color and a special but unseen spirit of Christmas.*

Here is what was happening. Each operator had upon their face an undeniable expression of satisfaction. Sewing machines were humming at full production, and the operators were intent on what they were doing.

The lessons learned that day are easily transferrable to the mind of almost any manager worth his salt.

A more recent example of the "family" culture that exists within our company involves a quilt. A very large quilt. So large, in fact, that *we believe it to be the largest signature wallhanging in the world.*

Quilting is a big thing in north Georgia. With all the quilt shows and quilting competitions in our area, we thought it would be appropriate to have a corporate quilt. So we cut quilt squares for everyone in the company and gave them each a square kit. We asked them to go home and create quilt squares that displayed their names and something about their role in the company.

We have over 500 squares in that quilt. It hangs in our cafeteria and provides another important stop on any plant tour.

We're proud of it. It is a stunningly beautiful construction which exists because we wanted to be part of something bigger than what we have to do at work every day.

I believe it's vital that companies look outside themselves for meaning and purpose. Usually the purpose already exists; we just have to recognize it and take some initiative. And that, in turn, can have remarkable consequences, inside and outside the company.

Because we market products for young children and infants, we were approached in 1990 to be a corporate sponsor for the Gainesville/Hall County Walk America. At the time, Walk America had limited involvement from the community, so we accepted the challenge to get on board. Bill Holbrook, Director of Human Resources at Warren Featherbone, established co-captains for the effort. The March of Dimes theme, "Walking for Healthier Babies," seemed particularly appropriate for our company.

That first year, our company had almost as many volunteers participate in the six-mile walk as the rest of the community combined. In 1989, the year before our involvement, there were 610 community-wide walkers. The following year 520 people from our company alone volunteered for the walk. Since that time, total community participation has grown to nearly 4,000 people who come from every walk of life and age group.

Because we manufacture children's clothing, our company has a specific connection with young children. We have a heartfelt desire to help babies be strong and healthy. Through our involvement with Walk America that desire has become our mission. Literally hundreds of people in our company took the initiative to help fulfill that mission, and as a result, led the broader community into a growing movement that brings hope and meaning to children everywhere.

The notion that the sense of family we have at Warren Featherbone can only exist in small companies is not true. One of the largest companies in the textile/apparel industry, and for many years one of our largest suppliers, has been Milliken &

Roger Milliken addresses the more than 3,000 "industrial heroes" inside the new Live Oak plant during an August 2 observance of the facility's rebirth.

Company, a family-owned business with approximately 15,000 employees. If ever there was a good expression of the "family spirit" within a large company, the experience at Milliken's Live Oak plant is certainly it.

MILLIKEN: THE LIVE OAK MIRACLE

On January 31, 1995, in less than a few hours, a major fire in LaGrange, Georgia, utterly destroyed one of world's best facilities for dyeing and finishing carpet. Milliken & Company's 700,000-square-foot, Milstar/Live Oak Plant burned to the ground. Without taking into consideration the cost of business interruption and other incidental costs, the fire's estimated damage was measured at nearly $200 million. The "family" of nearly 700 who worked at the plant were immediately confronted with a devastating crisis. What happened next could be called a miracle and a triumph of the human spirit. To fully understand what happened, one has to understand the company's background.

Milliken's Chairman and CEO, Roger Milliken, as an individual, has probably done more than anyone to help our industry discover our *connectedness*. During the eighties, our industry was experiencing a decline. We had a horribly inefficient distribution system. People who wanted to buy clothing would look for a particular size or color, but too frequently they would be disappointed. The system was not performing well.

Through Roger Milliken's efforts, the system changed. A new replenishment process was born called "Quick Response," in which computer linkages connected us to each other and enabled us to transmit information about what consumers actually wanted to buy. As a result, an entire industry improved its service to customers.

So Roger Milliken helped us discover our interdependence within the industry. Beyond that, he has helped the United States understand the role of quality and true excellence in what we do as manufacturers. "Crafted With Pride in U.S.A." was his brainchild. His company has won numerous awards and recognition for its leadership in quality, service and environmental issues. The list of his company's accomplishments is endless.

Milliken has also helped us better understand the responsibility that companies have in providing education to their people. The average Milliken management associate invests 40 hours a year in training through Milliken University. In terms of education per employee, it's a safe bet that Milliken does as much or more than any other company to provide education opportunities.

Through the Live Oak disaster, Roger Milliken and Milliken's president, Tom Malone, helped us understand yet another important principle related to interdependence, the principle of responsible leadership. The depth and speed with which the company's leadership responded to the fire has become almost legendary. Before the embers were completely extinguished, and before Milliken employees were given over to despair, they were making plans to rebuild. And without exception, within 24 hours, every employee was offered another job opportunity within the company worldwide. No one lost their job, or income, as a result of the fire.

The Live Oak story has other miraculous chapters to it. First of all, thanks to safety and environmental practices at Milliken, no one was injured and there was no contamination. Many companies, including competitors, offered assistance. In a fiercely competitive industry, two companies, Shaw and Mannington, actually helped Milliken manufacture carpet during the first few weeks following the fire. Think about that. What does it say about the positive cultures of those companies and the character of their leaders? What does it say about their respect for Milliken?

What makes the Live Oak story even more dramatic is its timing. Companies in the United States are experiencing massive downsizing and consolidation. They are moving offshore for manufacturing in order to decrease labor costs and increase profits. As a result, these businesses have helped to develop a perception that people are expendable, but profits are not. The idea that business leaders will do whatever it takes to get profits creates a lot of anxiety for everyone. Today, job uncertainty is a growing reality.

But Milliken's story runs completely counter to that perception. Priority was given first of all to safety. No one was hurt from the fire or any subsequent environmental consequence. No one suffered from loss of income, and although changes were inevitable, no one was left without opportunity to continue with the company. Nearly everyone did. There was never a question about Milliken's commitment to remain in LaGrange. People in the company and in the community received more than consolation. They found security.

On the surface, the Live Oak fire appeared to be a monumental disaster. It destroyed all *visible* means of support. But what it could not destroy was the *invisible* means of support, because that's where the real strength resides. It's only after we look below the surface of the events in LaGrange after the fire that we come face to face with a profound, life-transforming realization. Milliken's immediate decision to remain and rebuild in LaGrange was more than a reinvestment in Milliken; it was a reinvestment in many thousands of people beyond the company. It was a reinvestment in school systems, in libraries, public works, charities and scores of businesses everywhere.

In a very real way, Milliken reinvested in all of us! I'm personally humbled by the realization that their decision to rebuild was in fact an investment in the future, in our children and our unborn grandchildren. It was an investment that transcends our time. An act of faith that has made us all a little stronger.

Milliken & Company, like Warren Featherbone, has a history that dates back more than a century. The people who work at both companies share common heritages. Both companies are family-owned. Both have a stake in the same industry. But there's a reality more important than all of that. My belief is that neither company considers themselves to be a family business, but rather a business of families. The evidence of that is clear for all to see.

Still family after all these years.

Quick Response

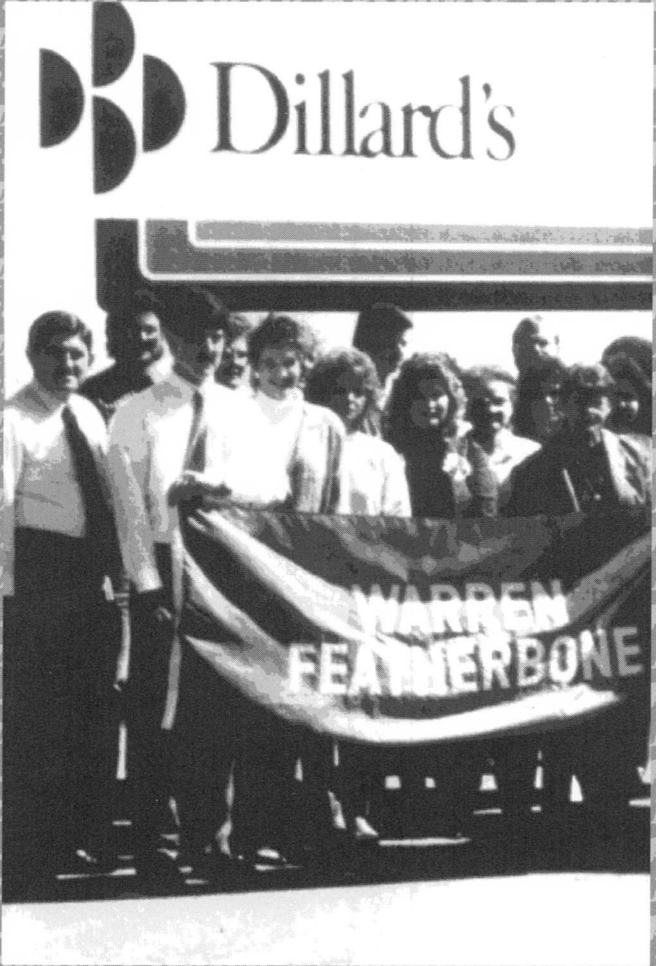

CHAPTER THREE

It's The Person, Not The Position

"A true leader helps us to move from where we are to
where we need to be and still enjoy the trip."

J. W. Fanning

University of Georgia

here are many heroes at The Warren Featherbone Company. So far, none of them have attained the worldwide
recognition of a Cal Ripken or a Mother Theresa, but their
achievements are no less worthy of our admiration. Within the
context of their own particular spheres of influence, they have
changed the course of history and positively affected the lives
of many people to whom they are connected. Space will not
allow all of their stories to be related here, but the following

account is particularly relevant to the message of this chapter.

A few years ago, Dillard's, a company with approximately 235 department stores, came to us with a challenge and a request. They wanted us to enter into a Quick Response program with them, whereby our companies would become connected through an electronic data interchange (EDI). EDI is a central component in the Quick Response process. Among other things, it facilitates reordering of products based on actual sales at the retail level. The benefit to consumers is the ability to find the right product at the right time and place.

As part of the program, Dillard's wanted us to deliver products within six days. At the time we were delivering product in about 45 days, with approximately 80% of items ordered actually shipped. I suggested that we begin with two products. I considered that to be a substantial commitment on our part and a rather brave response to their request. They said they thought "all products delivered within six days" was a better answer.

Soon afterwards, Ray Heflin, who was in charge of Dillard's Quick Response process, visited us in Gainesville and spoke to our supervisors about the issues facing retailers in today's marketplace. He described for us Dillard's desire to meet four primary objectives. They included having the same dollar investment while offering a broader assortment of products. They wanted their customers to be able to find products when and where they wanted to shop, and they wanted to eliminate mark-downs. These objectives are not peculiar to Dillard's, of course, but they relate to issues that are not always clearly understood by manufacturers.

People in our company began to see the larger picture, and we recognized that there were changes we could make to help us meet Dillard's requirements. Almost immediately, we set up a team to implement these changes, and several styles of our products were brought into the Quick Response process.

The program was successful, and it grew. For thirty consecutive weeks, we shipped Dillard's orders 95% complete within six days, meeting our objective without fail. Everyone was pleased with the success. But then came the week of Christmas. That year, Christmas Eve fell on a Tuesday, and we were scheduled to close. Since Dillard's transmitted orders on Sunday, we were left with only one day to ship orders, an impossible task.

Or so I thought.

In a discussion with our Quick Response team, I suggested that we request Dillard's not to transmit orders, as we didn't have time to ship them. Johnny O'Kelley, a supervisor in our shipping department, then asked a pointed question: "Let me get this straight and be sure I understand the Quick Response system. Will Dillard's be open this week?"

When I replied that they would be open, he continued,

"Well, it seems to me that if they are open and we don't ship orders this week based on last week's sales, Dillard's will be out of stock next week."

He was right, but <u>he</u> wasn't getting the point. I carefully enumerated the difficulties of shipping in one day. First of all, we would have to wake our computer operator in the middle of the night to travel 50 miles from north Georgia to start the computer program. We would have to prepare shipping tickets and locate all the merchandise. Then we would have to make sure that the Dillard's truck was here by 2:00 p.m. to pick up merchandise. All of this would have to take place on Monday.

Johnny O'Kelley responded by saying that he considered all those steps to be a good plan, and one we should implement at once.

Finally, <u>I</u> got the point. And we did implement the plan. We followed the script to the letter and made it happen. Our string of consecutive weeks of delivery remained intact through the holidays and into the summer. But then came the week of July the Fourth, when we traditionally close all week for annual inventory and vacation. Once again, I saw a problem with delivery, and I suggested that we ask Dillard's not to transmit orders. Re-enter our hero, Johnny O'Kelley, who said, "Let me get this straight and be sure I understand the Quick Response system." Then he asked the same question, "Will Dillard's be open this week?"

Dillard's was open that week, of course, but as I explained again to Johnny, it was an impossible situation. It had nothing to do with scheduling this time; it was an accounting issue. Historically, that was our week for taking inventory. We had done it for a hundred years, and we thought we were better at it than anybody. We had it down to an exact science. Not taking inventory that week would constitute a major change and create an inventory nightmare. Our accountants and management had agreed over the years to skip shipments that week to avoid the problem.

But Johnny O'Kelley's question motivated us to seek another solution. After all, we were paying the accountants to validate inventory; we could pay them to do it a different way. Ultimately, that's what we did, and we shipped Dillard's orders the week of July 4th. Now, as of the writing of this book, we've shipped 280 consecutive weeks — a total of 13,082 orders in the last year alone, averaging 97% complete. As far as we know, no other vendor has shipped product to Dillard's for more than 52 weeks straight, much less 280.

There have been further repercussions from the Dillard's story. The 97% completion rate led the way in setting new standards for order completion in our company. A few years ago, we might have been satisfied with 85% completion overall, but now we've improved our overall order completion rate to 95%. And thanks in large part to Johnny O'Kelley's leadership, we won't be satisfied to stop there.

I personally am not always a great leader, but I almost always recognize great leadership in other people. In my estimation, Johnny O'Kelley demonstrated leadership at its finest. It was heroic because he challenged the status quo and raised the pertinent question without fear. He trusted his instinct. He believed — and caused us to believe — that if we made up our minds to produce and fill the orders, we could do it.

Too often *we define leadership by the position*, but at its best, *leadership is found in the person*, not the position. In the Dillard's story, if leadership had come from the position alone, then the leadership that would have prevailed (mine) would have sent the orders back. But the culture within the company embraced the best solution to the problem, which didn't come from the nominal leader, but from the situational leader.

My friend, Rear Admiral Roger Gilbertson, has developed an interesting theory about leadership, drawn from his study of the history of mankind. He maintains that modern civilization, which comprises only a tiny percentage of man's time on earth, only helped to diminish our natural leadership abilities. He points out that during the hunter/gatherer period, leadership was widely distributed among all the people in each group. Someone hunting on the outskirts of the community, for example, was responsible for dealing with an intruder without returning to the group for instructions. The person closest to the situation assumed the responsibility of a leader and dealt with it. It was the natural thing to do.

I believe leadership still comes naturally. It is part of man's basic, inherent condition. Unfortunately, over the years we became "civilized" and perverted those basic instincts. Today's businesses are replete with people who are desperate to lead but think they are supposed to follow. And that line of thinking doesn't serve the best interests of the individual or the business.

A great part of my responsibility as a nominal leader is to allow people within the company to fully exploit their natural leadership capabilities. In many respects, that's what the empowerment movement is all about. But the empowerment concept can be a bit arrogant, if it communicates to employees, "You now have the freedom to think and act, and that is our gift to you." I suggest instead that what employees have to offer is a gift to the organization. What we should humbly be doing is releasing people to do what they are genetically built to do. The real breakthrough occurs when people feel free to lead, most often through quiet, responsible actions taken for the good of the organization.

The story of a plant supervisor in Michigan is a great example of individual leadership. A customer had called Buick to register a complaint and ask for a recall of his 1992 LeSabre. His brakes had gone out. Through an unusual series of events, Rich Richardson, a foreman at the Buick City Assembly Plant and a line worker, Michael Wilson, placed a call which went unexpectedly to the customer. In a career of approximately thirty years with General Motors, this was the *first* time Richardson had spoken directly to a user of his product. He felt the defect was so important that Buick "ought to tell him we are going to see that it never happens again." He explained to the customer that the responsibility was not management's, nor the Union's, but 100% his. Wilson also got on the phone to apologize that he had failed to bolt a brakeline bracket to a strut.

Several positive results evolved from this incident. First of all, Buick received a lot of valuable publicity about the improved quality of their automobiles. Secondly, an American automobile customer was ultimately satisfied that he had made the right decision to buy an American-made car. (He had previously owned a Toyota.) Finally, we all learned something important about leadership. To help spread the message in Rich Richardson's story, The Warren Featherbone Foundation presented him and the associates of the Buick City Assembly Plant with the Award for Excellence in U. S.-based Manufacturing. The ceremony took place on December 17, 1993 at the Buick

City Assembly Plant in Flint, Michigan.

If we realize that we all bear responsibility for leadership, very significant results occur. Like restoring faith in an American-made automobile. Or delivering a consistent product to a retailer for 280 consecutive weeks.

Rich Richardson (left) and Michael Wilson (center) receive the Warren Featherbone Foundation award at ceremony in Buick City Assembly Plant.

Johnny O'Kelley's story has been related over and over, through speeches and in written communication. Like Rich Richardson's story, it has taken on almost legendary proportions. They both have become celebrated heroes. But there are many others in our company and probably many at Buick whose actions qualify as heroic. Their leadership may often go unnoticed, but it is felt. And because it's there, the organization survives and prospers. These quiet heroes may be in charge of what appears to be the little things. They prove that leadership is not bound by their place in the company.

It's the person, not the position.

Mercantile Stores / Warren Featherbone and suppliers
Partnership Summit.

CHAPTER FOUR

In Charge Of The Little Things

"Reputations are both built and destroyed on small things."

- The Flint Journal, 1992

*Sh*ortly after the incident involving Rich Richardson's and Michael Wilson's apologetic phone call to a Buick customer, a *Flint Journal* columnist concluded that, "Some people probably consider what they did a small thing. And they are right. But then, reputations are both built and destroyed on small things." The two men at Buick were not in charge of the "big things" in their company, but they acted instinctively as leaders in charge of the little things. And their actions certainly had big consequences.

At Christmas time a few years ago, we received an unsolicited, but revealing letter from Mrs. Walburn of Muskegon, Michigan. Along with the letter, Mrs. Walburn enclosed a photograph of

her grandson, Alan. She just wanted us to know how pleased she was with our product and how well it had performed for Alan. She then continued to write that this particular garment was nearly 32 years old! It was from our 1959 line and had been worn by Alan's father and uncle.

Alan Walburn of Muskegon, Michigan wears an Alexis holiday article — produced 31 years before this photo. His uncle and father both wore it first!

At Warren Featherbone, we were struck with the significance of this letter and photograph. We imagined all the things that could have gone wrong with the garment: seams that could have ripped, buttons that could have separated, colors that could have faded. And yet, they didn't. We realized that

at least in one instance in 1959 we made the perfect garment and delivered 100 percent on the trust given to us by one of our customers.

The Warren Featherbone Company
Gainesville, Georgia 30501
USA

I'm In Charge of the Little Things

ALEXIS
USA

Following the receipt of Alan's photograph, we adopted a company business card that says specifically what everyone in our company does. Everyone has this card, which reads, "I'M IN CHARGE OF THE LITTLE THINGS."

I doubt anyone in our company understands the importance of the "little things" more than Nancy Flanagan. As the purchasing agent for Warren Featherbone, Nancy constantly deals with the details of our business. And her high standard of excellence in managing those details is unsurpassed.

During the eighties, major corporations and consultants were stressing the need for individuals within organizations to "think" (and thereby become rich and successful). Now we see that thinking alone is not enough. It implies that we give consideration to a particular facet of our job or business once and then move on to something else. Nancy Flanagan helped us understand and adopt a new way of looking at what we do. Working with others in our industry she emphasized the need for us to *"rethink"* the way we conduct our jobs, no matter how insignificant we may believe that job to be. She challenged us to find meaning in the mundane. Rethinking is an ongoing cycle of thinking and rethinking a process, skill or function until we reach a level of excellence.

Sparked by Nancy's inspiration, our company often "rethinks" many of the things we do in our business. One of the "small things" that has evolved into something very significant involves the way we visit our customers and suppliers and attend industry events. We take groups of up to 50 people from our company on state-of-the-art tour buses (complete with full audio and video capabilities) and conduct non-stop, "rolling" seminars. Our most ambitious bus adventure to date was a two-day trip to Cincinnati, the home of Mercantile stores. This was our first Partnership Summit with them, and we covered a lot of ground on that trip — in more ways than one!

The rolling seminar is a simple, but effective way to educate in an environment far removed from all distractions. Nancy's remarkable efforts at organizing these trips has earned her the affectionate title of Bus Boss.

GETTING TO ONE

As an airplane pilot, I have a great appreciation for the incredible skill and precision required to fly championship aerobatics. And no one is more precise in his routine than Leo Loudenslager, a seven-time aerobatic champion and extraordinary airshow pilot.

Loudenslager employs an interesting process preparing for a maneuver — a process that is useful to anyone who wants to reach a level of excellence in what they do. During a performance he has as many as twenty details he has to take into account. Initially, he has to take in the entire environment and consider the wind direction, air speed, engine power and all the other variables. As he gets closer to performing his first maneuver, he narrows his focus to ten points of concentration and lets the rest go. Then, as the power comes up and he releases the brakes, he focuses down to the five most important things he must remember. Finally, when he has the proper speed and he sees that the maneuver is a take, he narrows his focus down to two things, the initial pitch and the rudder input. All the rest is behind him. He lets it all go and concentrates on that one motion that will make the maneuver a success... the essence. At that moment, there's perfect alignment of his talent with the task.

I believe Loudenslager has learned the difference between competence and excellence. It's the ability to become so proficient with all the generalities — mastering the details — that we can now narrow our focus all the way down to the essence, the *"one."* Many times that essence is disguised as a seemingly unimportant thing, like the final stitch or application of color in a piece of clothing or choosing the right word to express a thought, but it's *only when we are able to master the details and "get inside the one" that we can reach excellence.*

As individuals we want to do big things, but most often we only have the personal power to do little things. But the more we take charge of the little things, the more likely what we do will make a big difference.

Remarks by Roger Milliken upon receiving the Warren
Featherbone Foundation Award during Georgia's
Manufacturing Appreciation Week 1996.

CHAPTER FIVE

The Real Key To Prosperity

"We have no more right to consume happiness without producing it than to consume wealth without producing it."
- George Bernard Shaw
(Candida, 1898)

conomically speaking, the United States today is a more polarized society than it has been in many years. Forty-two percent of the wealth in the nation is now held by only one percent of its families. We are becoming a nation where the rich are getting richer and the middle- and lower-income classes are becoming poorer. Overall, our standard of living is falling. In the last twenty years, the median household income has remained flat while the cost of living has risen significantly. That means that the average family's real wages have declined dramatically.

So where have we gone wrong, and what can we do about it?

I believe the answers are related to our growing inability to create wealth. Many economists believe that wealth is created in only three ways: through agriculture, extraction (mining, drilling, fishing, etc.) or manufacturing. Beyond those three, all other economic activities *transfer* wealth, but don't *create* wealth.

In recent years, this nation's ability to create economic wealth through manufacturing has been eroding. The apparel industry serves as a prime example. In the last 20 years, nearly two-thirds of our apparel competitors in childrenswear have gone out of business. But our industry is not alone. During that same 20-year period, 15 of 21 major manufacturing segments, as defined by the Department of Commerce, have developed trade deficits. The net annualized manufacturing deficit for these 21 manufacturing segments through June 1996 is $125.4 billion. This represents over 90% of the total trade deficit this year. As this deficit grows, so grows the outflow of wealth from the U. S.

Automation and robotics have contributed to the decline in manufacturing employment, but other factors play a larger, and more ominous, role.

First of all, there is the growth of lower paying service jobs. In spite of public perception to the contrary, manufacturing jobs

The Warren Featherbone Foundation

POST OFFICE BOX 383

GAINESVILLE, GEORGIA 30503

You're Connected!

These three books will tell you how.

No matter who you are, your life is made richer through your connection with the people in your family, workplace and community. These three richly illustrated books, with their positive message of recognizing the value of our "connectedness" make excellent gifts for those you care about.

And remember, it's for a good cause. These books are published by The Warren Featherbone Foundation, whose mission is to raise awareness of the importance of interdependent connections in business and in our personal lives.

Order for immediate shipping:

The Featherbone Spirit   Qty. _____

The Featherbone Principle   Qty. _____

Connecting The Generations   Qty. _____

Price – $19.95 each, plus $4.00 each shipping and handling. Orders of 10 or more books – no charge for shipping and handling.

Name _____

Shipping Address _____ Signature _____

City _____ State _____ Zip _____

Phone _____ Credit Card _____

Credit Card No. _____ Exp. Date _____

☐ MasterCard   ☐ Visa

JUST PUBLISHED

The Featherbone Spirit
– Celebrating Life's
Connections

The
Featherbone
Principle
– A Declaration
Of Interdependence

Connecting
The Generations
– Grandparenting For
The New Millennium

pay substantially more than service sector jobs. In fact, the 1996 average weekly wages in manufacturing were 44% *higher* than those in the service sector.

With the higher pay comes a higher standard of living, and not just for employees of manufacturing companies. There is the "multiplier effect", which means that for every job created in manufacturing there are many more created in other industries. Manufacturing operations depend on other suppliers and services, such as banking, insurance, shipping and transportation. Where a strong manufacturing base is developed in a community, the economy becomes very robust. It forces growth in other areas. On the other hand, when a manufacturing base leaves a community, the economy suffers.

Today, only 15.3% of total U. S. employment is in manufacturing. In 1979, it was 23.4%. More people are now employed in government jobs at all levels than in all manufacturing segments combined (Actual employment = Government: 18,398,000 vs Manufacturing: 18,234,000). What this really means in economic terms is that the United States has more people involved in wealth consumption than in wealth creation.

Another factor that has led to the decline of manufacturing has been the transfer of manufacturing jobs to other countries, theoretically to reduce labor costs. But there's a real problem with that line of thinking.

Recently, I received a call from a Philippines-based childrenswear manufacturer who had been in business many years. They were closing their operations and wanted to know if we were interested in buying their brand name. When I asked why they were liquidating the business, they responded that labor costs had risen to $5 a day, and it was killing them! What that said to me was that labor cost is not the major issue.

I believe one of the reasons many companies are sending jobs offshore is the result of a very narrow view of "cost." *Component* cost has become confused with *total system* cost. By total system cost, I mean all costs associated with the manufacture and distribution of products to the consumer. An apparent lower offshore labor cost may in fact contribute to a higher system cost, due to expenses associated with time and distance. The childrenswear manufacturer in the Philippines had an incredibly low component (labor) cost, but his cost of reaching his market was enormous.

Ironically, we are now seeing some high-tech *service* industry jobs (computer programming, for example) moving offshore to "low-cost" countries, such as India. If you think about it, almost everything is "cheaper" somewhere else if component cost is the only cost. But it isn't!

The question most often asked is, "Can the U. S. still manufacture products competitively on the world market?" The answer comes from a most interesting source: foreign business owners. The Germans, Japanese and other nationalities have already proven that products can be produced competitively in the U. S. using foreign labor — us! So the real question is, "Who will own manufacturing in the U. S., and where will the wealth that's created from it be invested?"

In my opinion, it's not foreign ownership of U. S. manufacturing, in and of itself, that causes concern. More significant is the fact that so many U. S. manufacturers have given up. And their giving up has left a vacuum which foreign manufacturers are more than happy to fill.

Other countries have already learned the lesson. They understand the importance of manufacturing to an economy. And they know that the real issue is *not* cheap labor, it's smart labor!

The United States has a clear need to rediscover the value of manufacturing and the connection between manufacturing and wealth creation. As a nation, we have taken manufacturing for granted, in much the same way we once took our environment for granted. Clean air and water were not an issue until we didn't have it. Before that we just assumed we would always have a clean environment. Then, when knowledgeable individuals and organizations realized we were in trouble, they heightened our awareness of the problem. Now, most of us are well aware of how fragile the environment is. But so too is our manufacturing sector. Its decline has already affected our standard of living, and its loss would be devastating.

So what can be done for U. S. manufacturing to make it more competitive?

First, we need to rethink the way manufacturing views itself and how it defines cost. We should look at cost in terms of meeting consumer expectations of quality, price and responsiveness. (In Chapter Six, this issue is further explored.) Secondly, knowledgeable individuals and organizations need to raise the consciousness of Americans about the critical nature of manufacturing in this country. People need to understand that we face a challenge to revive and maintain a strong manufacturing base. I believe we can meet that challenge.

In 1917, E. K. Warren created the Edward K. Warren Foundation for the purpose of *distributing* wealth. That foundation accomplished its mission, and today the people of Michigan are still the beneficiaries. In 1993, we resurrected the Warren Featherbone Foundation with a different mission: to help the United States better understand the need to *create* wealth through manufacturing.

The primary mission of the Warren Featherbone Foundation is to increase awareness of the importance of manufacturing in the United States. So far, the Foundation has helped to organize Georgia's first-ever, statewide Manufacturing Appreciation Week. A statewide group has come together to form *Georgians for Manufacturing*. It includes manufacturers, educators, chambers of commerce, the National Association of Manufacturers (NAM), the American Production and Inventory Control Society (APICS) and its Educational and Research Foundation, and other state manufacturing groups. Also playing a major leadership role in the formation of Georgians for Manufacturing is the Georgia Department of Technical and Adult Education in conjunction with the Georgia Department of Education and the University System of Georgia.

The Foundation has also made annual award presentations to various U. S.-based manufacturers, recognizing them for excellence in manufacturing. The 1994 award was made to the Buick City Assembly Plant in Flint, Michigan; the 1995 award was presented to The Boeing Company at their plant in Macon, Georgia; and the 1996 award was presented to Milliken & Company in LaGrange, Georgia. The 1997 award is being presented to Russell Corporation.

We believe it's important to create awareness and interest in manufacturing. Manufacturing has provided a substantial amount of wealth to this country in years past, and it will do so in the future only if we recognize its importance and the cost of losing it.

We believe it's crucial that our young people are educated about the importance of manufacturing and the career opportunities it affords. The popular image of manufacturing may be one of sweat shops with low technology, low skills and low pay. As a result, we are not attracting the best and brightest minds to careers that are in fact high technology, high skill, and high pay. These young people are the future of America and tomorrow's manufacturing leaders.

The Warren Featherbone Foundation has placed a specific emphasis on careers in manufacturing for students. Georgians for Manufacturing, with support from Georgia Power Company and other interested organizations, helped to print and distribute to thousands of high school and college students educational brochures which detail the opportunities available in manufacturing.

Like the environmental movement, manufacturing needs a movement of its own. It's an "economic" environmental issue and the real key to prosperity. We must preserve and protect it. When we do, we build America.

Reflections on the Warren Featherbone Foundation Ceremony during Manufacturing Appreciation Week 1996.

by Karen Schaffner — Publisher, <u>Apparel Industry</u> Magazine.

Among those who came to LaGrange that day were Georgia's Gov. Zell Miller and Trade and Tourism Commissioner Randy Cardoza. Lots of other politicians, educators and the press showed up. Gus Whalen brought a busload of associates from Gainesville. And Roger Milliken. And lots of his fans from LaGrange, of course.

When the tally was complete, there were well over 400 folks who packed an assembly room at the college. In true southern fashion, they sipped iced tea and chatted politely with their neighbors, admiring the decorations — thousands of red, white and blue balloons floating floor to ceiling in every corner of the room.

They dined on good southern cooking. And listened to the requisite welcomes from the organizers. Then things got serious.

How can I describe what that crowd was feeling? Remember how you felt when you watched America's athletes on the gold medal platform at the Atlanta Olympics? When they played the National Anthem and tears rolled down the cheeks of the winners? And your own eyes welled with tears of pride?

That's what it was like in LaGrange that day. For a few hours, 400-plus folks from all over Georgia came together because they share a deep belief in manufacturing and its role in America's future.

CHAPTER SIX

Who Is The Customer?

"In every implementation... of these types of partnerships and coordinating practices within the supply chain,
sales have gone way up and markdowns have gone way
down."

- Jan Hammond

(Harvard University, School of Business)

"All companies in the chain must realize that as long as
a consumer didn't buy, nobody has sold."

- Dr. Eli Goldratt

Author, <u>The Goal</u>

This Spring, on a visit to Seattle, I shopped at a store known
nationally for authentic American outdoor gear and apparel.

The store featured a good-looking, fairly expensive short-sleeved cotton shirt in their window display. I needed a shirt for summer, and I liked the color and the brand name. So I entered the store to buy the shirt. An associate in our company, Tom Wood, was with me. Once inside, we found that the shirt was out of stock in my size (small). I had to leave without making a purchase.

Before we left, we learned from the sales clerk that the shirts were made in Mauritius. I asked where Mauritius was located, but no one knew. In good humor, Tom told the sales clerk that since the store decided to have the shirt manufactured in Mauritius, there must be many Mauritians who shopped in their stores!

Tom had made his point, but I left without the shirt that I really wanted. I asked the clerk if she thought I could find my size in another branch store, but she said she didn't think so.

The following day, Tom and I were in San Francisco. I found another branch of the same retailer that carried the shirt. Although I have strong feelings about buying products made in the U. S., I wanted that shirt! We went inside only to find out that they also were out of stock in my size. So I suggested to the sales clerk that she sell me the shirt she didn't have and charge it to my credit card. When she found the shirt in my size at another branch or warehouse, she could send it to me. It was

May and I wanted a summer shirt. And I wanted *that* shirt, even if we had to have it sent from the manufacturer in Mauritius. (Mauritius is an island far off the coast of Africa in the Indian Ocean.)

The sales clerk said she didn't believe the plan would work, but she did have some helpful advice.

"Next year," she said, "you should come into the store earlier." When I asked why, she replied, "We always sell out of the small size first."

At that moment, I felt a wave of guilt. She had made it clear that I was the problem, because I came too late in the year! Although I wanted to buy that shirt, and surely they wanted to make the sale, it couldn't happen because I had waited too long!

THE APPAREL INDUSTRY'S DILEMMA

"We stumbled onto the obvious," someone once said. In the apparel industry, it seems we've done just that. We finally understand a basic principle that until the consumer buys a product no one involved in producing or selling that product (the value chain) has sold anything.

The value chain in our industry looks like this:

Pleasing the Joneses is not easy these days. They expect a lot before they become happy customers. First, before they will shop a particular retail store, it must be convenient and accessible. The store must have a reputation for carrying quality products. If they are buying one of our children's dresses, it must be the right design, color, and size. There can be no flaws in the stitching. And, of course, the price must match the value they place on the dress. If any of these criteria are not met, or if the Joneses are told they will have to wait a week or more for another delivery, there will be no sale.

Before the Joneses buy a dress for their daughter, that dress (or some part of it) passes through several companies in the apparel delivery chain. First, fiber producers convert raw material (cotton, for example) into fibers, which are then sold to textile manufacturers. They convert the fiber into cloth of different textures and colors, which is then sold to apparel manufacturers such as The Warren Featherbone Company. Using this cloth, we design and produce a finished product which is then shipped to a retailer.

The Joneses probably don't consider all the links in that chain of companies when they make their buying decision. It's unlikely that they evaluate the reputation of the fiber producer or the textile manufacturer before making a purchase. They probably will be more concerned with the manufacturer's brand name and the reputation of the retail store that attracted them in the first place. But the reality is that the quality of the dress they buy will be affected, for better or worse, by the performance of every link in the chain. The combined efforts of all the companies in the chain determine the value of the dress, and everyone's reputation is at stake.

So what happens when there is a weak link in the chain? What if the fiber producer supplies the textile manufacturer with poor quality fiber? What if the textile manufacturer delivers cloth three weeks late to the manufacturer? What if the manufacturer produces too many baby blue dresses and too few pink ones? What if the markup by the retailer is excessive?

Any one of these events affects sales at the retail level. If the

Joneses are unhappy, they will go somewhere else to get what they want. When that happens, everyone in the chain loses.

As simple as all that sounds, it's not something that has always been understood by companies in the apparel industry. For many years, the U.S. apparel manufacturing industry has experienced a serious decline. Much of the problem had to do with adversarial relationships between companies within the value chain.

For example, manufacturers sales representatives during the decades of the sixties and seventies developed poor reputations for salesmanship. Retailers perceived them as commission-hungry and only interested in the large, one-time order. And many were just that. Too frequently, manufacturers offered long lead times and low order completion rates. An 85% completion rate in 60 days was the norm. Then there were long delays in order approvals, which left the retailer ultimately with too much or too little stock. There were numerous other problems and very little sharing of information among the companies.

These and other weaknesses within the apparel/textile industry resulted in the loss of over one million jobs in the last 25 years, or approximately 40% of the entire industry. (Ten percent of all U. S. apparel manufacturing jobs were lost in 1995 alone.) There were large-scale changes in the retail industry also, including a significant number of corporate failures and consolidation. And, like it or not, we can't place all the blame for the problems on international competition. It's more a matter of not recognizing who are the real customers.

QR: THE ROAD TO RECOVERY

Since the mid-eighties, a significant movement in American apparel manufacturing has been Quick Response. The primary goal of Quick Response is to decrease lead times for delivery of product without loss of quality. Faster delivery provides a distinct advantage for retailers who can then offer customers the *right* products *when* they are ready to buy. When it's successfully implemented, Quick Response allows companies in a given value chain to have inventory readily available for delivery when the retailers place the order.

New technologies in electronic data linkaging support Quick Response by establishing fast, accurate communication between retailers and manufacturers. Bar coding and electronic data interchange (EDI) enable information at the point of sale to immediately filter back to all parties involved in producing and marketing the product. Companies down the line can better forecast what products they should produce. This, in turn, helps them keep their inventories at a manageable and affordable level, but still be ready to deliver products up the line.

Quick Response, as a concept, is wonderful. But for it to work successfully over the long term, *there is a catch.*

In its long history, The Warren Featherbone Company has gone to great lengths to provide the best quality merchandise possible. We've maintained high standards in our processes and materials to stay competitive nationally and internationally. But we haven't always been perfect, and still aren't.

In the late eighties, we were experiencing problems shipping product on time. As a result, we were on the verge of becoming a "weak link" in the value chain. Quick Response was leading the revolution in manufacturing, and we wanted to keep up. We didn't want to think about the consequences if we didn't.

Then several people in our company read Dr. Eli Goldratt's book, *The Goal.* Dr. Goldratt, an Israeli physicist and business strategist, cleverly explains in his book another breakthrough concept called the Theory of Constraints (TOC). TOC offers practical ideas for eliminating bottlenecks and improving throughput in the manufacturing process. We enjoyed the book immensely and saw its application to our operation. Once we understood these concepts, we went to work trying to implement them. Our on-time delivery improved immediately and continues to do so.

Knowing a good thing when we see it, a management group from Warren Featherbone later attended a seminar in Atlanta on the subject of the Theory of Constraints. One of Eli Goldratt's associates, John Covington, taught the seminar which again helped us better understand how to move product more quickly through our manufacturing operation. But we came away from the seminar with a new thought. If TOC could help a company improve its throughput, it could probably help an entire value chain as well. The issues we discussed at the seminar went beyond our company.

RETHINK CONFERENCE

To continue this new line of thinking, we organized what we called a "Rethink Conference." We invited all the members of our value chain, plus interested and related parties. They included DuPont (fiber producers), Milliken and Springs Industries (textile manufacturers), The Warren Featherbone Company (apparel manufacturers), and Mercantile Department Stores (retailers). Government was represented by the head of the Apparel-Textile Division of the U. S. Department of Commerce, and education was represented by universities with major textile and apparel programs.

At the time, Eli Goldratt's fees for one day were too much for our small group to absorb. But we wanted him there. John Covington intuitively sensed that we were on the verge of a breakthrough and convinced Eli Goldratt that this was an opportunity to speak at once to an entire industry about his theories.

Rethink Conference with Dr. Eli Goldratt.

So he came. And the conference was a knockout. Everyone left with the realization that something extraordinary had happened. We were onto something, and we knew we should continue the process. What evolved was a series of meetings with Dr. Goldratt at Clemson University, coordinated by Ed Hill, site director at Clemson Apparel Research. Over a 12-month period in 1992, project teams from each of our companies met to discuss the implications of TOC on an entire value chain.

What we discovered was that the value chain is very inefficient in providing consumers what they want, when they want
it. Quick Response was the goal, but for it to work, all members
in the value chain had to buy in. One of the primary reasons is
that the value chain is only as strong as its weakest link. An
inefficiency or lack of quality by any one company affects the
overall speed of delivery or quality of the product at the retail
level.

We also looked at the other major problem that has developed in the industry over many years — "hot potato" inventory.
All businesses that produce products know they must move
their inventory as quickly as possible on to the next level in the
chain to avoid the costly prospect of keeping it. It has become
a dangerous game where the company that ends up with the
most inventory in the chain, loses. As a result of this, the relationship between members of the value chain has often been
adversarial.

Then there is the issue of transfer pricing, where components are marked up in price several times before the consumer
buys them. Each company in the chain thinks of the next link in
the chain as its customer, without regard to the ultimate customer, the Jones family. And the Joneses aren't willing to pay
for all that markup!

What we learned at the Rethink conference is that all the companies in the value chain can help themselves by thinking more holistically. None of us have revenue until the Joneses make the purchase. Until that point, all we have is expenses. Instead of links in a chain, each company becomes a part of one integrated supply system.

This alignment of companies we now refer to as QR^2 (Quick Response to the second power). It's also known as the "virtual integration of the system," a term coined by Jan Hammond at the Harvard Business School.

The idea behind virtual integration is that each company in a value chain behaves as if it is one part of a whole company. It changes the way we relate to one another in very specific ways.

One example of how this new relationship occurs involves one of our suppliers. We've committed ourselves to buying all of our terry cloth from them, which allows them to dedicate all of their output from two machines to Warren Featherbone, 24 hours a day. We even have our company name painted on the machines. So the operators who work on those machines work for the entire supply chain. We get weekly deliveries, whereas five years ago we would have deliveries once a month. A major head start toward Quick Response.

Virtual integration means we think about our suppliers and customers in a different way than we have in the past. The tangible results of being virtually integrated can be rewarding. Consider the "Story of Pink."

THE STORY OF PINK

One of the major links in our value chain is Springs Industries, a quality textile company. For many years, they have provided fabric to The Warren Featherbone Company. In the mid-eighties, they were a leader in Quick Response and helped us understand the value of it. We established a series of meetings with them twice a year to discuss issues that affected the way we conducted business with each other. Even at that point, we were experimenting with the idea of thinking like partners rather than adversaries.

During one of those meetings, we took members of the team from Springs Industries on a plant tour. One of the team members, Joe Berger, noticed that we were stockpiling large quantities of cloth, and he asked us why we were doing that. It was a bold, provocative question, because we were buying all that cloth from Springs Industries. He had good reason not to ask the question, but he was genuinely interested in helping us make better buying decisions.

We explained to Joe that part of the reason for so much cloth inventory was the color pink — five shades of it! We thought that we needed all five shades of pink in order to meet consumer demand. But when we took a closer look, we all realized there was little variation from one shade to the next. Collectively, we decided to reduce the five shades to one, substantially *reducing* our inventory.

Before this meeting we were carrying too much inventory. The reduction broke a bottleneck in our manufacturing operation, and affected our bottom line in a very positive way. The benefit to Springs could only happen if our total business improved, which it did. Delivery of five shades of pink required five SKUs (stock keeping units). It was harder for them to ship that many variations. When they cut it back to one, their business with Warren Featherbone *increased* by 40%!

QR^2, the virtual integration of the system, works. Because of the Rethink Conference, the companies in our value chain have developed an entirely new and radical way of partnering together. We think as one, because we understand more fully our interconnectedness. Our delivery times and the quality of our products have improved dramatically. The apparel industry, when it thinks of itself as one company, can provide retailers and consumers a "value" that literally can't be beat anywhere in the world. We can compete!

QR∞ — Rethink II

The Rethink Conference was a breakthrough event, but it was just the beginning. We realized that if QR^2 worked for the apparel industry, it would work in other industries that have similar alignments. And since we are all indeed interdependent, since we share common suppliers, distributors, retailers and consumers, shouldn't we share what we've learned?

So we organized another conference, "Rethink II", and invited businesses from other industries. The conference was held at Clemson University and included businesses and representatives from the luggage industry, the transportation industry, and the housewares industry. We centered the conference around another major issue — forecasting — relevant to all companies who produce goods. Forecasting, in simple terms, is the process of determining in advance what your customer is going to want later.

So we focused on forecasting. Each company presented its forecasting methods and the results it was achieving. Some, like Samsonite (the number one producer and marketer of luggage in the U. S.), were very sophisticated, using marvelous mathematical models which predicted consumer behavior. Others, like The Warren Featherbone Company, were relatively crude. We were simply looking at past sales and basing our estimates for the future on that information.

What we discovered, however, was that regardless of the level of sophistication of our forecasting methodologies, the results are basically the same. In the end, we have no idea what consumers will actually do and there is practically no way to make predictions. On top of that, because of our electronic linkages, we discovered that, in terms of forecasting, we were getting wrong answers faster. The electronics provided these wrong answers in more visually pleasing forms — pie charts, bar graphs, etc. — but they're still wrong. And we can't run our businesses based on the information they provide.

We now understand that the ultimate forecast is the sale of the item in the store. To truly know what the customer wants, and therefore what we should produce, we have to determine how to respond so quickly to reality that we are producing for reality.

The Rethink II conference provided a forum for members of value chains in different industries to discuss our commonalities. Common problems and solutions. Common goals and relationships. And, of course, common customers.

What we took home from the conference was an expanded version of virtual integration that went beyond the limited scope of our particular value chain. The new model looks like this:

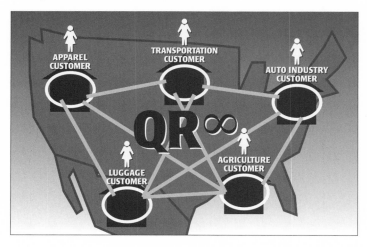

The basis for QR∞ is interdependence. When we understand that our different businesses, and our different industries, are all interconnected, we break the old paradigms that have constricted us. In the end we *can* please the Joneses. And we can make them happy without looking for our labor forces overseas. This is how America competes — interdependently.

Quick Response will work, *but there is a catch*. It can be summed up in a word: trust. To put an end to adversarial relationships, we have to look at other businesses in our value chain — and other industries — as our trusted partners. We have to think and act as partners who win together.

Trust can be found in the largest organizations. JC Penney is the world's largest seller of children's clothing, but even with their enormous size, they still bring a "win-win" approach to working with their suppliers. Along with many other large department stores, they are setting an example and proving that it *can* work.

Trust. Working together as if we are partners. In the final analysis, as we attempt to compete on an international level, it may be our best hope.

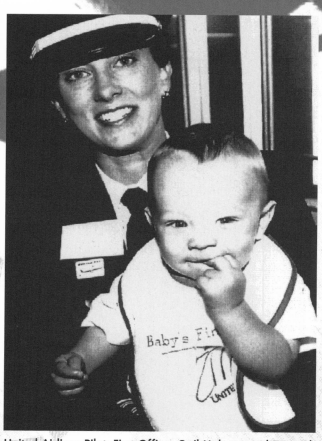

United Airlines Pilot, First Officer Gail Holmes, and 7 month old son, Grant, at the Washington/Chicago Inaugural 777 Flight, June 7, 1995.

CHAPTER SEVEN

No One Flies Alone:
A Declaration Of Interdependence

"Concern for man himself and his fate must always form
the chief interest of all technical endeavors."

- Albert Einstein

It seems that everything about The Boeing Company can be described as large. Their product is large. The Boeing 777, for example, weighs 535,000 pounds, about 534,999$\frac{1}{2}$ pounds heavier than our latest product at Warren Featherbone. Their plants are large. The largest, located in Everett, Washington, covers an area the size of 90 football fields. Since the jet age began, Boeing has manufactured 60% of all commercial airliners produced. Every day, Boeing jetliners carry 2.5 million passengers, which adds up to 675 million people a year — 12% of the world's population! As a single manufacturer, Boeing has annual revenues equal to about 60% of *all* the apparel produced in the U.S. by approximately 20,000 manufacturers.

These are but a few of many astounding facts regarding Boeing's size. The statistic that holds the most significance for me, however, is this:

Boeing employs over 100,000 people and works directly with about 30,000 domestic suppliers. By contrast, The Warren Featherbone Company employs about 500 people and works with about 225 domestic suppliers.

So what does a giant like Boeing have in common with a small baby clothes manufacturer in Gainesville, Georgia?

Actually, there was a time in our company's history when we were directly linked to Boeing. During World War II, when Boeing was manufacturing airplanes for the war effort, Warren

Featherbone was a direct supplier of machine gun belts. That supplier relationship ended after the war, but our companies are still very much connected.

Careful reflection on that "connectedness" reveals a couple of astonishing facts: By virtue of the size of Boeing's work force and supplier network, there's no other company in the U.S. with more people who directly buy baby clothes from Warren Featherbone. And Boeing jets probably carry the majority of families — parents, grandparents, aunts, uncles and children — who buy and wear our clothing.

Our company has a stake in the success of Boeing. As long as they exist, they are a significant part of our customer base. And, if they carry that many of our customers (and our employees), it's directly in our best interest that their airplanes are the safest in the world. Likewise, Boeing has a stake in our company. The more successful we are, the more airplane tickets we will buy.

Boeing's power base lies not just within their own company, but also with the interdependence it enjoys with thousands of other U. S. companies, including Warren Featherbone. We all have common customers and suppliers. We have common problems, such as massive consolidation within our industry segments. We have common challenges in supplying consumer demands. We have a common system of government support or non-support. We have common hopes and dreams for our employees. Boeing's prosperity supports ours. Our prosperity supports theirs. *The United States as a country will be able to compete internationally only through our ability to leverage this interdependence.*

In 1995, The Warren Featherbone Foundation presented The Boeing Company with the second annual Award for Excellence in U. S.- Based Manufacturing. We wanted to recognize them for yet another significant statistic about their company: For five consecutive years prior to receiving the award they were ranked as the United States' number one exporter of manufactured products.

The award ceremony took place in Macon, Georgia, where Boeing's half-million-square-foot facility employed nearly 800 people. On hand were a number of Boeing representatives, including Phil Condit, President of the Seattle-based company. His comments to the assembly were insightful and inspiring, and he was quick to give credit to the employees who were directly responsible for Boeing's success as a Georgia manufacturing concern. Building a huge jet aircraft requires the collective effort of many people, and Phil Condit certainly understands that.

But the comment that especially caught my attention came after the ceremony during a conversation in the press room. I recounted to Phil how I first became aware of Boeing's presence and the company's philosophy. It had happened at a conference in North Carolina, I told him. Just a chance meeting with one of Boeing's officials. Phil Condit's immediate response gave me pause: "There are very few chance meetings."

There are very few chance meetings, because when we stop and think about it, we are all connected in some way. This is a vital concept that, fully understood and incorporated into our lives, can help us reach our potential as individuals, and as

Gus Whalen and Phil Condit at the kick-off luncheon for Manufacturing Appreciation Week in Macon, Georgia.

companies and industries. The alternative to this concept is *isolation*. It's my opinion that isolation can lead to any number of problems in our society, including alcoholism, drug addiction and suicide. *Interconnectedness,* on the other hand, fills one of man's greatest needs: *to realize that we are not alone.* There's great comfort and assurance when we have people who are there to support us.

At the awards ceremony in Macon, I delivered a speech that

I entitled, "A Declaration of Interdependence." Boeing's award was intended to be a message, a declaration, that we are at our best when we realize our interdependence. On a large scale, Boeing represents the possibilities available when we leverage our connectedness. When Boeing says, "No One Flies Alone," they honestly understand what they are saying.

The March 1995 awards ceremony in Macon greatly increased our understanding about interdependence. But that's not the end of the story.

A few months later, in June, Boeing was scheduled to launch their 777 aircraft. I wondered if there was a connection there, a way for Warren Featherbone to support them in that. We developed an idea for an embroidered baby bib that would read, "Baby's First Flight" and presented it to Boeing.

Boeing loved the idea, but since United Airlines was scheduled to be the launch carrier, they thought we should contact them. Our idea was to include United's logo on the bib and give a few of the bibs away on the inaugural flight — all in the spirit of recognizing and promoting U. S.-based manufacturing.

We sent sample bibs to the promotions department at United and waited for a response. A week before the inaugural flights (seven of them to various cities), we received word from our contact that United thought it was a great idea. They wanted bibs for all seven flights and invited me to join them on one.

This bib has been especially designed and manufactured by Alexis for the inaugural flight of the United Airlines 777. Alexis infantswear is manufactured by The Warren Featherbone Company, Gainesville, Georgia, USA, now in its 112th year of continuous operation. Alexis infantswear is sold through fine department stores and specialty shops in North America, Europe and Japan. We salute United Airlines and The Boeing Company for the great achievement in US-based manufacturing represented by the 777.

We hope you will enjoy this Alexis bib and the inaugural flight of the United 777. With best wishes from the people of The Warren Featherbone Company.

C.E. Whalen, Jr.

C. E. Whalen, Jr.
President and CEO

UNITED AIRLINES

Baby's First Flight

UNITED AIRLINES

Suddenly we had a rush job on our hands, and we worked overtime to produce the bibs. We managed to produce about 50 bibs for each flight. We felt that would be enough for all passengers with a baby in the family.

On my flight, after we were in the air, the head flight attendant read my note to the passengers, which was printed on the hang tags of each bib. She then pointed out the various features, including colors, texture and design. When she finished, we distributed the bibs but exhausted our supply while we were still in First Class. To our surprise everyone wanted a bib. The remaining passengers sensed there was something amiss, and realized we were in the midst of a bib shortage. They went into a bib frenzy!

The irony of that scenario was immediately apparent to me. Here we were, 32,000 feet up in a brand new $125 million jetliner, but people were anxious to get their baby bib. They seemed transfixed with the idea of flying aboard an aircraft built for the "next generation," and the bibs provided a tangible way to connect to that next generation. Getting their hands on one of those bibs had now become imperative.

To soothe the crowd, the flight attendant announced that those who still wanted bibs could write me a note and we would send them one. Before I left the plane, I had 148 notes from people all over the world. The farthest away was Australia and the closest was Athens, Georgia. We shipped the baby bibs out to them within a week.

But that's not the end of the story.

With each bib shipment, I asked the recipients to send me photographs of their babies, whether they were children, grand-children, nephews or nieces. Within a few weeks they poured in. Using those photographs, we designed and produced a 1996 calendar, featuring Babies of the Inaugural 777. Again, it was a big hit, and it helped promote the idea that our companies were connected to each other and to our customers.

But that's not the end of the story, either.

Since many of the photographs came from grandparents, aunts and uncles, we were reminded of how important the ex-tended family is in raising our children, particularly today when there are so many single-parent households. Another idea ger-minated, then blossomed. To support and honor the role of grandparents in the family, we developed a joint promotion with United Airlines. On the anniversary of the inaugural flight, United Airlines awarded 32 sets of round-trip tickets to families in the United States who shop in stores that carry our Alexis brand of infantswear. The catchphrase on the counter cards in each participating store was, "I want to see Grandma and Grandpa."

As far as I know, this promotion is the first of its kind in our industry. Its success will be measured over time and not just in terms of dollars. My hope is that we are speaking to people about our interdependence. Family members need the support of other family members. With the maturation of the baby boom generation, there are more and more grandparents. They have an opportunity to help pull their families together, and we want to support them in that.

That's still not the end of the story, I'm certain, but where it ends, we don't know. Someone once told me that an idea, rooted in good, will flourish. This story, which began with a "chance" meeting, has evolved into something very significant. The business story has its place, but the real significance is the message. It's a large message. Like Boeing.

No one flies alone.

TOBU SPIRIT
店 是

GOOD SERVICE
顧客第一（奉仕）

GOOD CHALLENGE
創意工夫（進取）

GOOD COMMUNICATION
一致協力（和親）

CHAPTER EIGHT

Tip From Tobu

"The Black Ships have come again!"

- Kan Yamanaka

The United States has always wanted to do business with Japan. So much so that, in 1853, President Fillmore sent a naval expedition there with instructions to open Japan to foreign trade and diplomatic contact. A year later, on a second visit by Commodore Perry and his fleet of black ships, the Edo bakufu signed a treaty of friendship.

Perhaps the United States, along with most of the Western nations, were a bit overzealous about free trade, but the treaty did mark the beginning of Japan's modern era. Within a decade, Japan, for centuries a decidedly closed nation, became an open book. In 1868, power was transferred from the Tokugawa shogunate to a young emperor, Mutsuhito, and the city of Edo became the city of Tokyo, the "eastern capital." The Meiji Restoration had begun.

Today, Japan is a world trade leader.

Consider the following:

• According to *Fortune* magazine, the world's three largest industrial and service companies (ranked by sales) in 1995 were all Japanese (Mitsubishi, Mitsui, and Itochu). Ten of the top 15 were Japanese! Japan's commercial banks hold 8 of the top 10 spots when ranked internationally by assets.

• The country has just 49% of the population of the United States, but 66% of our Gross Domestic Product (GDP). So Japan's per-capita GDP is $33,701, compared to $25,009 in the United States. The only country with a higher per-capita GDP is Switzerland.

• 23% of Japan's workforce is employed in manufacturing, compared to 15% in the United States. Japan's manufacturing sector accounts for approximately 28% of the country's GDP, versus 20% for the United States (and 33% for Europe).

Japan didn't attain its position in the world market by accident. There's a general belief that in the United States, we tend to welcome people from other places, but not new ideas. In

Japan, it's just the opposite. Not only are they very receptive to new ideas, but they aggressively seek them out. When the Meiji Restoration first began, Japan realized they were far behind the rest of the world, so they imported knowledgeable people — scientists, engineers and businessmen — who could educate them and guide them into new technologies and better ways of conducting business.

The Japanese realized that to compete, they must learn from others. And they more than succeeded. For many years, we looked down on Japan as a nation that only knew how to copy others. Today we have a better understanding and greater respect for their approach. We've even developed a name for it: *"benchmarking."*

A few years ago, a couple of benchmarking champions from Japan made contact with us. Mr. Kan Yamanaka, President, and Mr. Koichi Nezu, Executive Vice President, of Tobu Department Stores, have always been strategic thinkers. Through the years, they have paid attention to retailing in the United States, because most of the broad changes in the Japanese retail industry generally are led by the U.S. The rise of supermarkets, and later the rise of discounters, are events that in some way or another have occurred in Japan, usually a few years after they occurred in America.

Sometime in the eighties, when many American department stores were struggling to survive, Tobu's leaders saw an opportunity for learning. If they could determine what was causing some department stores to fail and others to succeed, then possibly their company could leapfrog those problems when they inevitably made their way to Japan. Their interest in American retailing practices had nothing to do with wanting to conduct business in America. They simply wanted to gather ideas and learn new technologies which could be applied to their business in Japan.

Specifically, Tobu wanted to better understand how the value chain in the United States was benefitting from the use of the Quick Response process. Working through a Boston-based consulting firm, Next Frame, Inc., Tobu's leaders established dialogue with Dillard's, and through them The Warren Featherbone Company. But what started as a learning adventure evolved into something much more significant.

From the beginning, we were honored to be a part of the dialogue. Tobu is no small chicken. Their office/retail complex in downtown Tokyo covers about eight acres and contains more than three million square feet of commercial space. The Tobu store alone comprises more than a third of that. That's about the size of an entire shopping mall in America!

There are two basic types of retail stores in Japan. One is the older, more established store, which started years ago by selling traditional Japanese items (kimonos, for example). The other type is a post-World War II phenomenon referred to as the terminal department store. Terminal stores such as Tobu were developed by owners of railway transit companies. With millions of people passing through their terminal stations everyday, the railway companies found a way to capitalize on all that pedestrian traffic by developing retail stores around the stations.

The Tobu Department Store is perched atop a major Tobu railway station. 2.83 million people pass through the station everyday! It's no wonder that Tobu takes in more income from that one store than an entire division of a typical department store chain here in the states.

So we began the process of exchanging ideas with representatives from Tobu. In spite of our size difference, they were genuinely interested in how we were doing business within the value chain. And there was no commercial interest, just a desire on both of our parts to learn from each other.

THE BLACK SHIPS HAVE COME AGAIN!

During the time we were sharing ideas, someone suggested that maybe Warren Featherbone could sell the Alexis line in Japan. The immediate reaction from Tobu was caution. They knew as well as we that there were many obstacles to overcome for us to do business together. They didn't want to make promises about products that they couldn't keep. And we were not ready to make promises about delivering products halfway around the world.

A month later, Tobu's Boston consultant, Bernice Cramer, met with Mr. Yamanaka and Mr. Nezu in Japan. She reviewed with them what was learned from Tobu's meetings with us and other companies. In the process, she showed them a few Alexis dresses from our holiday line. To satisfy his curiosity, Mr. Yakanama asked Bernice to tell him the retail price of the dresses. His guess was in the neighborhood of $150 to $200. She told him that they were retailing for about $30 to $35.

At that point, Mr. Yamanaka pushed back his chair and exclaimed, "The black ships have come again." He was amazed that we could produce the quality product he now held in his hands for such a good price. To him, we were Commodore Perry reincarnated, but our cargo was pink and baby blue. Suddenly, he was interested in more than a dialogue with us. He wanted to do business.

Today, the Alexis line is sold in Tobu's downtown Tokyo store, as well as a few of their other stores. We were the first company to establish an electronic data interchange system between their company and the United States. Tobu is learning about Quick Response firsthand.

There were several people from Warren Featherbone who worked hard to insure our newfound relationship with Tobu would be successful. George Murphy, head of management information systems at Warren Featherbone, established the electronic linkage between the two companies. George had pioneered the

Alexis-Link connection to Baby Superstore, February 12, 1987. (L-R: Linda Robertson, Jack Tate, George Murphy and Gus Whalen)

"Alexis-Link" system earlier with a forward-thinking customer of ours, Baby Superstore. That system connected a Baby Superstore PC with our mainframe for the purpose of electronic transmission of purchase orders. The system George developed for Tobu was similar, so we gave it the name Alexis-Link International.

Initially, Tobu had called in a consultant for the job but were told it would cost $30,000. George went to work and provided the system at no cost to Tobu — a substantial savings and a good start to the relationship.

To work successfully with Tobu, everyone who is part of our manufacturing operation had to make significant adjustments, from purchasing to customer service to manufacturing. Many of the requirements for producing overseas called for standards for sizes, material and labeling that differed from ours. For the relationship to work, we had to do more than just adapt to a few changes. Yvonne Whitmire, our head of customer service, developed a slogan about change, and today it hangs in our conference room:

> ## ACCEPT CHANGE – GOOD
> ## EMBRACE CHANGE – BETTER
> ## CREATE CHANGE – BEST!

With Tobu, we didn't just accept change, or even embrace it. We created it.

ALEXIS . . . U. S. A.?

We wanted to see photographs of our Alexis shop at Tobu's main store, so our friends at Tobu sent us a few color photographs that included signage of the store. When we studied it,

Alexis shop in Tobu Department Store, Tokyo, Japan 1996.

we noticed a change they had made in our logo. They had added "USA" under the Alexis brand. We were surprised, but after some thought and discussion, we realized that it made a lot of sense. They added "USA" to the logo because they thought it enhanced the brand name. We realized that if they considered it an enhancement, maybe we should consider it an enhancement as well. So now we're Alexis USA.

Our relationship with Tobu continues to grow. We have swapped interns with each other, and we are improving our product and delivery to them. They are long-distance partners. Their openness and their sincere desire to learn from others has led to something beyond our expectations. Something we all profit from.

I found it interesting to learn about Tobu's stated, threefold mission, particularly the third part. First, they stress "good communication". Like us, they have learned the value of staying connected, both internally and externally. Secondly, they stress "good service", because they recognize the importance of happy customers.

Finally, they stress "good challenge." There is great significance for us in those words. Just as we did in years past, Tobu has found opportunity in crisis situations. They welcome challenge, and in recent years there's been plenty of it in Japan. Consumers there are following the path of consumers here by relying more and more on their own abilities to choose and judge quality. To them higher price does not necessarily mean better quality. They want value.

What Tobu has already learned from us is the need to become more efficient and the need to bring value to their products. Understanding those two important needs, particularly the latter, has led them to a better understanding of their role in their industry. No longer do they think of themselves as isolated from the rest of the value chain, acting more like a selection committee choosing from a pool of hungry vendors out to rip off the consumer. They don't have to have adversarial relationships with their vendors, if together they can discover their interdependence.

The value chain in Japan is much more complex than it is in the United States. In terms of relating to members of the value chain, Tobu faces many more challenges than most retailers face here. But their experience with Warren Featherbone gives them a successful relationship to which they can point. Many of the people at Tobu thought it was a crazy idea to do business with us, and it's certainly not a huge merchandising venture. On both sides, it has consumed a lot of people's time and energy. But, if the business equation doesn't make perfect sense, the sharing of ideas and learning from each other certainly does.

ANOTHER ORIENTAL TALE

Tobu is not the only experience I've had with the long-range view found in Oriental retailing. Many years before I met the wonderful people there, I had a personal encounter with a shirtmaker in Hong Kong. It was a small transaction in 1970 that eventually turned into a big lesson in retailing.

That year my wife, Nell, and I took a full year's savings and traveled to the World's Fair in Osaka, Japan. We stayed for a while at the Mandarin Hotel in Hong Kong, and I visited a store called David's Shirts, Ltd., in the basement. It was the thing to do if you were traveling abroad, so I had three shirts made. The total cost for all three was $11, a reasonable price, even though the quality turned out to be less than satisfactory.

That purchase occurred in July. The following Christmas I received a card from David. Considering it was only an $11 purchase, I thought that was very considerate. A year later I received another card at Christmas, and I thought that was truly remarkable. Today, more than a quarter of a century later, I still receive cards from David at Christmas time. He has not missed a year yet.

David's kindly persistence can teach us a valuable lesson about serving customers. I wouldn't be surprised to see a David's Shirt Shop one day in downtown Gainesville, just because he knows the value of staying close and staying in touch. We tend to take customers for granted. Realtors make house sales in the hundreds of thousands of dollars and the buyer may get a one-time thank you for the business. Automobile dealers do the same. But 26 years after an $11 sale, David is still saying thank you.

THE ORIENTAL CONNECTION

Thanks to his annual thank you card, I still feel connected to David's Shirt Shop. And our relationship with Tobu has brought Japan to our very doorstep. We're taking a deliberate step toward recognizing our interdependence, although we're thousands of miles away from each other.

Tobu and other Japanese businesses have a unique understanding of interdependence. Many years ago, compared to the rest of the world, Japan was weak economically. Now they are strong. Their tremendous economic strides have come from their ability to leverage their interdependence, corporately and personally. Now it's time for us to re-learn how to do the same.

POSTSCRIPT:

In July of 1996, Tobu's Executive Vice President, Mr. Nezu, and his wife, visited our company in Gainesville. He brought with him some very good news. In a meeting with about thirty people in our management group, he explained that during the first eighteen months of our relationship with Tobu, the retail store had sold virtually every Alexis product delivered to them. Furthermore, they had not received a single return for defects. Not one.

Then, in appreciation for the partnership and everyone at Warren Featherbone who helped make it possible, Mr. Nezu announced that Tobu was making a significant financial contribution— a three-year commitment— to the Warren Featherbone Foundation.

It's wonderfully ironic that Tobu recognizes the importance of U. S. manufacturing.

RS, we p

workmanship sou

will be aware of the needs of

for attractive, well-fitting,

ble and safe garments.

IL CUSTOMERS, we pledge

ently high-quality products sol

price, which can be re-sold at a

for our retailers. We further p

cient sales support, order hand

d delivery.

EMPLOYEES, The Warren Feat

ompany believes that the "fam

our business has helped to p

we have enjoy-

CHAPTER NINE

A "Step" Toward Interdependence

"We have to advance trust before we earn it."

After my father died in 1969, The Warren Featherbone Company experienced significant changes in leadership. People in the company, as well as people in our industry, quite naturally were concerned about how those changes would affect them. The company, like apparel in general, was struggling, and there was speculation that it might be sold.

I knew speculation had led to rumor when I received a call from a representative with *The New Yorker* magazine wanting specifics. He told me he had it on good authority that we were being sold.

"I got it right from the horse's mouth," he stated.

I explained to him that he could consider me a horse, and we were not selling the business.

The significance of that incident was twofold. First, it proved the power of an unfounded rumor. I still have no idea how the false report made its way to a magazine in New York. Secondly, the realization that I was "the horse" was a wake-up call. Suddenly, I saw more clearly the overwhelming responsibilities that loomed in the immediate future.

My father had been very well-liked. And with good reason. He was an honorable man, whose values were self-evident and consistent with the way he raised me. We all missed him. What was left in his wake was a degree of confusion and uncertainty about the future. We were facing a tremendous challenge — certainly the greatest yet for me in my early career.

From that point on, each Sunday night, I went to bed with thoughts of the coming week. I looked at the days ahead as chaos that somehow would have to be managed. There were too many unknowns, challenges I wasn't sure I was prepared to meet. With all that weighing on my mind and the week ahead of me, I didn't sleep well.

Today, after thirty years, I still don't sleep well on Sunday nights. The struggles haven't gone away, and they never will. Struggle is constant. And I don't believe that success is defined so much by what you achieve as it is how well you deal with the struggle.

Nor is chaos the exception. It's to be expected. Anticipated. And, if you are really excited about your life, welcomed.

In medical vernacular, the idea that you have reached ultimate rest is called "flatlining." You're not just resting anymore, you're dead. If you study graphic readings from an electrocardiogram, you notice a significant difference between flatlining and "normal" life. A good heartbeat has regular peaks that create radical surges above the "flatline."

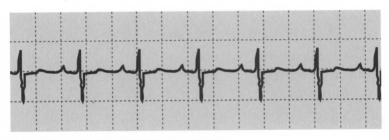

DIAGRAM OF NORMAL ECG

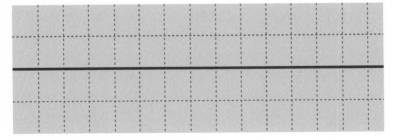

FLATLINING = DEAD

So chaos and struggle, like the blips on a heart monitor, are constant. If we're not struggling, not experiencing some degree of chaos in our lives, we're flatlining. With that in mind, if we choose to live, the issue then becomes learning how to best deal with that constant.

A great help in dealing with the struggles is recognizing our interdependency. Drawing on others for support reduces the weight of life's challenges and responsibilities. The load is lightened. Discovering my interdependency with others certainly has helped me better handle the responsibilities I've faced through the years, and I hope I've helped others. As a company, Warren Featherbone has benefitted from working interdependently within our industry and community.

Our company expresses its interdependence through our Corporate Creed. This Creed spells out clearly the responsibilities we have to seven segments of our society. Fundamental to our relationship to these groups is the basic premise that fair and honest dealings are a cornerstone on which all relationships should be built.

CORPORATE CREED

TO CONSUMERS, *we pledge consistent high quality and workmanship sold at a fair price. We will be aware of the needs of customers for attractive, well-fitting, comfortable and safe garments.*

TO RETAIL CUSTOMERS, *we pledge consistently high-quality products sold at a fair price, which can be re-sold at a fair profit for our retailers. We further pledge efficient sales support, order handling and delivery.*

TO EMPLOYEES, *The Warren Featherbone Company believes that the "family image" of our business has helped to produce the success which we have enjoyed for over 100 years. People make the company, and not vice-versa. In view of this, Warren Featherbone intends to manage the business in a caring manner, providing the best work conditions possible, fair compensation, job security and the ability to advance according to one's initiative and talents.*

TO SUPPLIERS, *The Warren Featherbone Company desires to promote a professional partnership with the suppliers who provide for our manufacturing needs. Our responsibilities include the expectation to receive the highest-quality products and our willingness to pay a fair price for same. Our intent is to continue the same long-lasting relationships with our suppliers that we enjoy with our retail customers.*

TO THE COMMUNITY *in which Warren Featherbone operates, our intent is to be a good corporate citizen, paying our fair share of local taxes and providing for significant and stable employment. We further wish to contribute the leadership of the members of our Company to civic affairs, to provide funds for worthy organizations and in every way, to be a good neighbor.*

TO THE ENVIRONMENT, *Warren Featherbone pledges not only its desire to be a pollution-free producer, but also to help better the surroundings in which its facilities are located. We feel the responsibility to build attractive buildings compatible with the local environment and preserve beauty in every way that we can.*

TO LOCAL, STATE AND FEDERAL GOVERNMENT, *Warren Featherbone pledges itself to be a responsible participant in government. We feel the need to be aware of the workings of government, provide leadership where called upon, to respond constructively to government programs as they are initiated. We expect to pay our fair share for government services and in every way to be loyal as a corporate citizen of the country which has given us the free enterprise system.*

The Corporate Creed is timeless. Although it was developed in the early eighties, it could have been written over a hundred years ago. The company's history proves it has always lived by these commitments. And we've always understood our interdependence with these seven segments of society.

Taking The First Steps

So how do we make interdependence happen? We can't, but we can allow it to happen. And there are at least two prerequisites that open the door for interdependence.

First, look for areas of common interest with other people, businesses or organizations. Consider your common issues, your common goals, values, or needs. They are always there. Then, once those commonalities are identified, they become the basis for the relationship. They are the ties that bind.

Secondly, risk being vulnerable in areas where knowledge or expertise is lacking. The first condition for learning is to realize that you don't know something. We don't have all the answers. Admitting it advances trust, and *we have to advance trust before it's earned.*

One of the legendary stories from our company's past involves Louis Simons, who met my great-grandfather in the late

1800s. Simons was still in his twenties, but already a successful merchandiser on the West Coast. The two men shared their common interests, goals and challenges. They learned from each other. They developed a business relationship totally based on trust. During his 53-year association with Warren Featherbone, Simons never had a contract nor a bond, though he made collections for the company running into the hundreds of thousands of dollars.

In 1906, San Francisco experienced a devastating earthquake, which left thousands of people and businesses in dire straits. Louis Simons had developed a large customer base for Featherbone products in the area, and many were about to experience severe financial crisis after the quake destroyed their homes and businesses. The Warren Featherbone Company wrote every customer in San Francisco and cancelled the balance due on their accounts. The letter explained that they owed nothing; that the company wanted to help them get back on their feet. The partnership between Louis Simons and Warren Featherbone was that strong!

Obviously, we can't be partners with everyone, and there has to be a degree of selectivity involved. That's where intuition can help. Our intuitive sense is probably much more powerful than we realize. *If it feels right, it probably is.*

And there will be conflict in relationships. Conflict is natural. It's like chaos — something you can expect. But recognizing our interdependency and building relationships based on trust provide a framework for dealing with conflict. It requires some hard work at times, but the rewards are well worth the effort. E. K. Warren built a relationship with Louis Simons based on trust and a spirit of partnering together. That relationship brought a lot of revenue into our company years ago.

Today, we enjoy many "partnering" relationships that are proving to be just as rewarding. In recent years, both Sears and the Belk stores have held their centennial celebrations. It's gratifying for us to be able to say that our relationships with both those companies spans most, if not all, of those hundred-plus years. Talk about long-term relationships!

The idea that we have to advance trust before we can earn it is not new with me. Thanks to my parents, I came to understand the concept when I was very young. My father provided his children with unconditional acceptance and love. He was also very wise and intuitive, as evidenced by his marriage to Doris, my stepmother.

Doris married my father when I was 10 years old. We were strangers to each other, and she was faced with the challenges of bringing two families together to form a new, larger family. As a stepparent, it would have been easy, maybe even expected, for Doris to maintain a certain distance from me. And vice versa.

But we didn't. We gave each other trust before we earned it. That provided us a wonderful framework for our relationship to prosper through the years.

In 1969, our relationship evolved to another level when we were both thrust into leadership roles in the company. Any business relationship has its share of challenges, and ours was no different. But again, because we had developed a great degree of affection and trust for each other, we were able to grow through those challenges.

Stepparents should be honored for the contribution they make to the lives of their stepchildren. Unfortunately, they frequently don't get the credit they deserve. Our culture doesn't always provide much encouragement or support. But "stepping" in as a parent is a selfless act and one of the most important of our day. There are more than 35 million stepparents in the U.S. Clearly, there is a great need to understand their crucial role.

Parenting your own child is challenge enough. But stepparents have an extra mountain to climb. Too often, they are perceived to be threatening or indifferent. Those perceptions create the wrong foundation for a parent-child relationship. They lead to adversarial interaction. Trust, on the other hand, will lead to greater trust and love for each other. It doesn't come easy, but in time it will come, if at least one of the parties is willing to take the first step.

Throughout our company are many examples of people who have deliberately "stepped" into the role of parent. Some are stepparents and others are foster parents. They have made heroic personal sacrifices by bringing literally hundreds of children into their homes and loving them as their own. These same people bring that remarkable spirit of giving into our company, and I believe our company is better for it. What we do as individuals affects who we are as a group. We all relate to each other a little differently because of their commitment.

I believe there are special places in heaven for stepparents. Undoubtedly, they've learned something that others haven't had the opportunity to learn. Undoubtedly, they've learned how to advance trust and earn it.

Life is a struggle. To think otherwise is foolish. But if we discover our interdependence with others, if we take the first step of trust and allow it to happen in our lives, that struggle has meaning. For all of us.

危机

CHAPTER TEN

The Spirit Of Interdependence

"We should consider ourselves as spirits having
a human experience, rather than humans having an
occasional spiritual experience."

- Teilhard de Chardin,

20th Century French philosopher

Interdependence. For some of us, the idea flies in the face of what we've been taught. Like John Wayne, aren't we stronger if we're independent, self-sufficient, and fearless? In business, can't we be more competitive if we aggressively beat our own path to the top? The truth is, we try to compete in a world where the most successful of our competitors are not that way. For the most part, they all work in alliances. They don't think of business (or life, in general) as necessarily "win-lose". They believe in and practice, wherever possible, "win-win."

Discovering our interdependency in our personal and business lives doesn't just affect us in a social sense, although there are certainly positive social ramifications when we do. Interdependence, understanding that we are all connected, is a spiritually-based concept. Its well-spring is spiritual.

I learned about this spiritual dimension through a family crisis a few years ago. Shortly after the crisis came to a close, I was invited to speak to Hall County's first community-wide Mayor's prayer breakfast, sponsored by a group of Gainesville businessmen. The event was fashioned after the National Prayer Breakfast in Washington, D.C. I considered entitling my presentation, "I'm In Charge of the Little Things," based on the Alan Walburn story told earlier in Chapter Four. In the process of preparing my remarks, however, I discovered a much deeper meaning. The content of that message follows:

Have you ever thought that we live in times of crisis? Did you see last night's newspaper? Did you see last night's paper ten years ago. Here were the headlines:

- **Arab leaders adopt a peace plan**
- **GBI says state officials may be involved in wrong-doing**
- **Hall County jobless rate has reached 9.5%**
- **Local Chamber of Commerce short on money**
- **Georgia colleges bemoan budget cut order**
- **Image hurts congressional veterans**

Seems as though crisis continues. It involves every area of life. Perhaps we need a new way of dealing with crisis.

A good friend of mine in California sent me these Chinese symbols for crisis:

The two symbols together translate the word "crisis", but the meaning is very different from the one that Americans normally associate with this word.

The Chinese see crisis almost as growth, or transition — something that should be expected. We tend to see crisis as limited in time, something to be endured, something to get beyond — kind of like getting beyond the current economic crisis.

The top element in this Chinese word translates literally into our language as the adjective "dangerous." The bottom element translates into the more significant meaning of the two, which is "opportunity." Oftentimes we see the danger in crisis, but we over-look the opportunity. Perhaps that's why the headlines don't change.

I had an opportunity to re-learn this special meaning in cri-sis through an experience which began for me and my sister Margaret on Christmas Day. On that day, she called me to say that she did not feel well and that perhaps we needed to go to the hospital.

We did, and the testing began. Approximately ten days later, after a complete MRI exam, she and I were seated in her doctor's office to hear the results. The results were devastating. Margaret had inoperable brain cancer, and life, as we know it, was lim-ited to a matter of months.

I relate this story not because of the personal and family tragedy involved. For many, many people have endured the pain and suffering that was encountered. And if you are going through something similar, I now understand personally what you are experiencing, and my heart goes out to you. I mention this story because of something Margaret said to me that reminded me that there is opportunity, even in this crisis.

You can imagine the silence as the two of us rode home to-gether in the car. Not knowing what words of comfort I might

*offer, I asked Margaret this question: "If our situations were re-
versed and I had just been given your diagnosis, what would
you say to me?" I was surprised how quickly Margaret responded
to my question.*

She said, "Gus, I would tell you this:

> *- Hang in there.*
> *- God works in strange and wondrous ways.*
> *- Most importantly, there are many things in life worse
>   than dying."*

*What I learned was that although we can't really do much
about the timing of our death, we <u>can</u> do a lot about those things
that are <u>worse</u> than dying — things that separate us from each
other. Things like the way we treat one another, our families, our
business relationships and our basic relationship with nature
on this earth. Margaret felt these things are worse than dying
because they diminish life and are <u>preventable</u>.*

*Beginning on Christmas Day, I spent part of nearly every
day with Margaret for the next seven months up to and including the day that she died, August 12. I learned another very
powerful lesson. Though I saw her deteriorate physically, I also
saw her spiritual strength grow tremendously. It reminded me of
the thought which a friend of mine passed along not so long ago*

that "we should consider ourselves as spirits having a human experience, rather than humans having an occasional spiritual experience."

Our real strength is spiritual, not physical. That's what lasts and can be developed as we age. We spend a good deal of time preparing ourselves physically in health clubs like the one in our city, Fit For Life. Maybe we should be thinking of developing ourselves to be fit for eternal life. I suspect that if we're not fit for eternal life, we're really not fit for life either.

The good news is that, if we grow spiritually, we are coming together and not falling apart as we age. Margaret was and is a very strong spirit. I miss her, and I miss the wonderful example of love that she set for my family and the many people who knew her.

So here we are assembled today in the first meeting of this type ever in Gainesville — a prayer breakfast. We are saying thanks to each other for being who we are and looking to our Maker to help us live the kind of life that brings peace and joy and harmony. We are trying to find the opportunity in crisis, and, in a variety of areas, solve big problems. But as individuals, we cannot solve big problems. All we can do is work on the small but very powerful components.

This reminds me of something we learned at the Warren Featherbone Company. At Christmas time, we received a photo-

graph of a little boy, Alan Walburn. Alan's grandmother sent us a letter along with the photograph, in which Alan is wearing one of our Holiday velveteen outfits. Mrs. Walburn is from Muskegon, Michigan, and she told us how pleased she was with our product and how well it had performed for Alan. She then went on to say that this particular garment was nearly 32 years old! It was from our 1959 line, and had been worn by Alan's father and uncle.

At Warren Featherbone, we were struck with the significance of this letter and photograph. We began to think of all the things that could have gone wrong with this garment — seams that could have ripped, buttons that could have separated, colors that could have faded. And yet, they didn't. We realized that at least in one instance in 1959 we made the perfect garment and delivered 100 percent on the trust given to us by one of our customers.

Following the receipt of Alan's photograph, we adopted a Company business card that says specifically what everyone in our company does. Everyone has this card, which reads, "I'M IN CHARGE OF THE LITTLE THINGS."

As individuals we want to do big things, but we have to realize that we only have the personal power to do little things. If they are done well consistently over time, very significant results occur — like the garment that lasted over thirty years.

When we came in this morning, we symbolically checked

our credentials at the door. I'd like to suggest that we leave them there, permanently. Those credentials tend to separate us from who we really are. Instead, I'd like to suggest a new business card for every one of us. This business card indicates specifically what we can and should do in life... the only things that will have lasting meaning: "I'M IN CHARGE OF THE RIGHT THINGS."

It's the right things that we do, often in small quiet ways, that enables us to find opportunity in crisis; grow spiritually and avoid those things in life that are worse than dying; and in all ways, be worthy of the One who sent us here in the first place.

Thank you for being a part of something that I believe our community will remember as one of the right things. The greatest asset of our community really has nothing to do with geography, natural resources, or industrial base. It's the spirit of our people. Thank you for who you are — especially at a time like this.

The Mayor's Prayer Breakfast
Gainesville, Georgia

I'm In Charge of the Right Things

_____
Signature

That first Mayor's Prayer Breakfast was a remarkable event. It was spearheaded by James Mathis, a visionary banker and superb organizer. The Georgia Mountain Center, where it was held, was packed to capacity.

The event had the drama of a Billy Graham crusade, in that people came expecting something special. The Gainesville area had experienced its share of political and cultural tension in recent years, and the people in attendance were politically and culturally diverse.

By all rights, I should have been nervous about my role as keynote speaker. Margaret had passed away less than a month prior to the prayer breakfast. When I sat down to write my message, it literally came in a matter of minutes. It was an experience that somehow seemed orchestrated by someone other than myself. I was no more than a messenger.

The message itself was reprinted by the *Gainesville Times*, then later reprinted in part by *Guideposts* magazine, under the heading, "Pass It On." From that small excerpt in *Guideposts*, which was printed on the last page of the magazine, we received over 1600 letters asking for reprints of the entire message. We are still receiving letters as this book goes to press in 1996. The letters come from virtually every state in the country and a number of foreign countries. They are signed by people from every walk of life, from college presidents to prison inmates.

Three years after the prayer breakfast, we received a series of letters from a pastor in Southern Leyte, The Philippines. He had read the article in *Guideposts* and was struck by the message, "I'm in charge of the right things." His church, New Frontier Presbyterian, printed the slogan on T-shirts and used them in a fundraising effort. With the significant profits from that venture, the church was able to continue a church building construction project.

Now, when I look at samples of the T-shirts which Brother Pacha sent us, I am reminded that this message was "passed on" to thousands of people all over the world as a result of a crisis situation — my sister's death. There is a clear lesson in this for us all, and it's this: Expect and understand crisis. There are seeds of opportunity in life's saddest moments. Our challenge is to help them grow.

But there may be a larger message and one that hopefully gets to the core of what this book is all about. That message is what we call the Featherbone Principle. Because we are all connected, all that we are and all that we do does affect the world around us. All the heroes mentioned in previous chapters have made their business environments, their communities and their families better places to live and work. They have accepted their responsibility to do the right thing. They've taken charge of the little things. They've learned that there are times when it's good to be vulnerable and advance trust so it can be earned.

We're not alone in this world. Whether we recognize it or not, there is an interdependency that exists for us all — corporately, socially and spiritually. The sooner we discover that reality, the better for us all.

This is our declaration of interdependence.

The Warren Featherbone Company

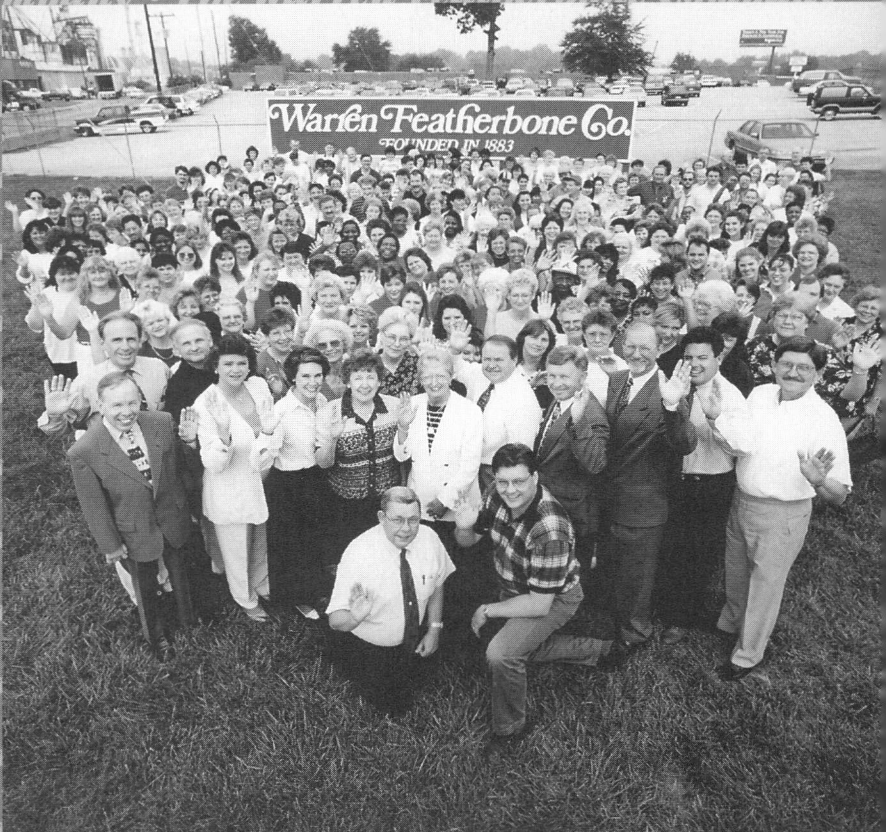

or The Heroes

The Warren Featherbone Company has succeeded because it has transcended a family business to become a business of families. Throughout the years, thousands of people have made Warren Featherbone their family business. They have provided the company with creative energy, intellect and renewal that has kept us young.

Evelyn S. Dunagan, our treasurer for nearly forty years, exemplifies these qualities. Her dedication to the company and its people reflects the spirit of today's Warren Featherbone heroes listed below:

Betty J. Adams	Patricia L. Anderson
Mildred Adams	Wendy D. Anderson
Jan H. Adkins	Helen J. Arroway
Arlene Ahlers	Jo Anne C. Ash
Doris L. Aikens	Jane R. Askew
Eula J. Aikens	William A. Atkins
Evalena S. Aikens	Etta M. Ayers
Amanda Alexander	Joyce A. Ayers
Alisha L. Allen	Vivian M. Ayers
Annaree Allison	Adellar M. Bagwell
Eva L. Allison	Karen L. Bagwell

Ricky D. Baker

Eloise P. Baldwin

Dana D. Ballew-Jordan

Kimberly L. Barnes

Lila E. Barnes

Elsie Barnett

Miriam Barrett

Tracy M. Barrett

Maria L. Barron

Cindy Bates

Carolyn S. Bearden

Robert J. Bearhope

Renee Beatty

Stephanie Beatty

Barbara J. Beavers

Barbara J. Beck

Mildred L. Benson

Teri A. Benton

Patricia A. Bloomquist

Geneva A. Boggs

Robin S. Bohannon

Elizabeth A. Boleman

Marjorie E. Bollinger

Ruby J. Bolton

James B. Bond

Stella Booth

Patricia Bowman

Donna V. Bradshaw

Audrey N. Brady

Sandra M. Brantley

Gail Breazeale

Misty Breazeale

Lorene Brewer

Opal Bridges

Kristy M. Britt

Agnes K. Brock

Jennifer Brock

Polly A. Brockmon

Martha G. Brooks

Phyllis A. Brookshire

Marcell Brown

Viola L. Brown

Shirley Browner

Elise D. Bruce

Linda S. Bruce

Donna A. Bryant

Connie D. Bryson

Earsell H. Buffington

Barbara A. Buice

Carol S. Bulgin

Bruce Burch

Glenda G. Burrell

Renee Burt

Dorothy E. Butler

Patricia E. Cabe

Christy D. Cagle

Hazel J. Cagle

Carol L. Cain

Knox Campbell, Jr.

Eva L. Cane

Virginia D. Cannon

Nellie K. Cantrell

Sabrina Cantrell

Lisa Cao

Debbie L. Carder

Gearldean G. Carder

Dorothy N. Carter

Yuvonne C. Carter

Sue Chadwick

Suzanne F. Chalekian

Yong M. Chambers

Elaine V. Chandler

Mildred Chandler

Jennifer L. Chapman

Patricia A. Chastain

Tommie L. Chastain

Brenda C. Cheek

Lori A. Childers

Georgia F. Childs

Benson J. Clark

Doris D. Clark

Elise Mae Clark

Hazel E. Clark

Kelly M. Clark

Wendy S. Clelland

Jean M. Cole

Carolyn Collins

Elizabeth Collins

Elba Contreras

Timothy V. Copp

Annie P. Corn

Brian K. Corn

Kevin Corn

Audra M. Crane

Willie M. Crisler

Tammy Cronic

Sandra J. Cross

Gregory Cruce

Phyllis S. Cruce

Essielene Crumbley

Nery Cubur

Laura E. Dale

Robin D. Dale

Betty J. Daniel

Rosetta Daniel

Jacquelyn W. Deal

Joyce I. Dean

Michael H. DeGrave

Blanca Delgado

Lurene G. Denton

Melissa Dodge

Theresa Diaz Polo

Brenda C. Dover

Maria M. Dubnik

Patricia A. Dubnik

Ann E. Duck

Maudie E. Duckworth

Latashia Dukes

Evelyn S. Dunagan

Montrella A. Dunagan

Sharon M. Dwyer

William H. Dyal

Mary E. Dyer

Melissa Dyer

Richard S. Eckard

Ann E. Edwards

Betty R. Edwards

Myrtle L. Elliott

Carolyn S. Ellis

Harold Ellison

Marjorie Elrod

Charlotte F. Emmett

Maribel Ensenia

Lisa Escoe

Loretta Escoe

Betty S. Evans

Nancy M. Evans

Ann N. Ferguson

Brian Ferguson

Dorothy Fields

Mary J. Fields

Jimmy D. Flanagan

Nancy A. Flanagan

Pamela D. Floyd

Arzellia Franklin

Carol S. Freeman

Bessie J. Fuller

Tammy L. Furgerson

Carol Gage

Wanda J. Galvan

Margarita Garcia

Aleida Garza

Christine Gee

Carla R. Gibbs

Sonya J. Gilmer

Crystal M. Gooch

Betty S. Gowder

Kim M. Gravitt

Wanda S. Greene

Ken Greenwald

Mary L. Grimes

Lucille G. Grindle

Sherlon P. Grindle

Shirley R. Grindle

Alice K. Grizzle

Betty M. Grizzle

Doris E. Grizzle

Satilla B. Grizzle

Dortha L. Grogan

Eva H. Grubb

Charlotte B. Gunter

Wayne H. Hackler

Sandra E. Hamby

Cynthia Hamilton

Nae M. Hammack

Mary Louise Hardman

Deborah E. Harkins

Michelle L. Harris

William T. Harris

Kinue O. Head

Tammie L. Helton

Penny K. Hemrick

Sheryl A. Hendrix

Armando Hernandez

Catherine R. Hicks

Cora E. Hicks

Melinda C. Hicks

Sara J. Hicks

Leisa A. Highfield

Clint T. Hill

Lori A. Hill

Toan Ho

No Hoang

Bertha Hogan

William T. Holbrook

Lunell P. Holcombe

Linda E. Holder

Paula D. Holloway

Ruth Holman

Geraldine Holman

Herman H. Hooper

Janice E. Horne

Anna Howah

Christopher S. Howard

Lorine Howard

Vernelle B. Hubbard

Mary Huff

Elise S. Huffstetler

Amy M. Hulsey

Billy D. Hulsey

Donna K. Hulsey

Johnie W. Hulsey

Valerie K. Hulsey

Sherry J. Humphries

Dale R. Hunter

Kimberly A. Hysong

Dixie Ingebrightsen

Jacqueline M. Ingram

Geneva Irvin

Sandra Jackson

Jesse D. Jamerson

Leigh S. Jarrard

Vivian S. Jarrard

Cassandra L. Jenkins

Mary C. Jenkins

Faye C. Jett

Barbara H. Johnson

Clara U. Johnson

Dorothy A. Johnson

Edna C. Johnson

Mary A. Johnson

Mary J. Johnson

Mattie G. Johnson

Wayne E. Johnson

Barbara C. Jones

Cynthia Jones

Edna R. Jones

Gail B. Jones

Jenny M. Jones

Kathy J. Jones

Lee Ann Jones

Mildred Jones

Queenie E. Jones

Timmy B. Jones

Linda L. Jordan

Mario R. Julaju

Margaret S. Kelley

Ronald K. Kellner

Mildred B. Kelly

Penny I. Kendall

Amber Kent

Penny E. Kerns

Edgar N. Kerr

Margaret L. Key

Dorothy E. Kierbow

Linda H. Kincaid

Linda J. King

Mary A. King

Tammy R. King

Martha J. Kinsey

Mary A. Kirby

Christy L. Knight

Crystal A. Krich

Allene F. Lane

Mahala G. Langford

Theodora M. Laws

Betty Ledbetter

Eva J. Ledford

Jerry L. Ledford

Ollie J. Ledford

Janet R. Lee

Troy Lingle

Marilyn B. Lipscomb

Joyce A. Lockaby

Alberta Long

Julius E. Lord

Virginia Lord

Pauline J. Lovell

Karen M. Lynch

Janice MacDonald

John F. Macke

Nadia W. Mady

Christy L. Maloch

Dana M. Manning

Wanda R. Marion

Barbara Martin

Charles K. Martin

Mary L. Martin

Wanda Martin

Alma Massingale

Helen J. May

Jackie Y. Mays

Shelby McCannon

Tammi L. McClellan

Jeanette S. McClure

Joan E. McClure

Charlotte L. McDaniel

Geraldine McDougald

Boyd L. McEver

Rebecca A. McKee

Cecile B. McMillan

Frances M. McNabb

Ann M. Michael

Carol A. Miller

Emma L. Miller

James C. Miller

Katherine J. Miller

Wanda E. Miller

Selina E. Millsap

Stella W. Millsapps

Juanita M. Mintz

Estelee S. Mooney

Melissa K. Morris

Deborah A. Morrison

Jimmie Moss

Latrecia Moss

Linda J. Motes

Gwen Mullinax

Sharon R. Mullinax

George H. Murphy

Marilyn Murphy

Marsha L. Murphy

Misty A. Murphy

Lisa P. Nash

Lois V. Nash

Melissa F. Nash

Patricia T. Nation

Ruth Nation

Judy Nasmith

Mang T. Nguyen

Thu Lang Nguyen

Dora G. Nicely

Pearl F. Nix

Tammy L. Norris

Carolyn F. Northrup

Johnny E. O'Kelley

Rosa B. O'Shields

Lucy Ogden

Audrey R. Ogle

Rachel S. Oswalt

Albert A. Oliver

Joe Palant

Yvonne A. Parker

Thena L. Parks

Carol G. Parson

Omazell L. Parson

Ruth M. Passmore

Jagruti M. Patel

Manoj C. Patel

Patricia A. Patrick

Christi E. Patterson

Kimberly Patterson

Loy C. Payne

Amy Pearson

Beverly L. Peck

Carolyn A. Peck

Ira M. Peck

Mary D. Pepper

Sandra G. Perkins

Karen Perry

LaRue B. Pethel

Judy S. Pettyjohn

Ha T. Phan

Thelma Pierce

Melinda A. Pitchford

Ruie Pittard

Connie E. Posten

Larry R. Potts

Joy A. Power

Marilyn F. Pressley

Beth A. Pruitt

Sue L. Puckett

James Purdy

Wayne L. Quintana

Nancy Ramirez

Catherine Ramsey

Melody J. Ray

Wanda E. Reagan

Wanda K. Redmon

Brandi L. Reed

Dorothy C. Reed

Amanda F. Reeves

Irene S. Reeves

Mildred Reynolds

Mary Rhinehart

Kay E. Richardson

Sheila L. Richardson

Kathy M. Rider

Wanda P. Rider

Quinn Riordan

Rika Riordan

Gregory W. Roberts

Sandra A. Roberts

Bobbie V. Robinson

Cynthia L. Robinson

Eva B. Robinson

Jacqueline E. Robinson

Jerry W. Robinson

Marina Robinson

Sherry Robinson

Rosa E. Rodriquez

Donna J. Rogers

Heather B. Roland

Judy Rollins-Gowing

Stan Rollins

Norma A. Rosales

Elaine B. Rouse

Teresa D. Rundles

Cathy B. Russell

Christie Russell

Betty Ryan

Ana Sanchez

Mary J. Sanders

Ann E. Sargent

Laura J. Satterfield

Mildred I. Saxon

Kathy Saylors

Nancy Schlichting

Martha Scott

Carol Scoggins

Carol G. Scott

Opaline W. Seabolt

Carolyn Shepherd

Steven M. Shiplett

Bonnie J. Shipley

Vicky S. Shoemake

Florence M. Skinner

Tamatha K. Slay

Susan J. Smallwood

Betty J. Smith

Bonnie Smith

Deborah A. Smith

Elsie Smith

Gail M. Smith

Margarette L. Smith

Perry R. Smith

Ruby A. Smith

Ruby V. Smith

Wanda D. Smith

Rose M. Snow

Alice M. Sorrells

Phyllis T. Standridge

Carla Statham

Annie B. Stells

Latres E. Stephens

Lunette M. Stover

Marsha L. Strickland

Kevin M. Stuhler

James Summerour

Charles N. Tanner

Fannie E. Tanner

Dan Tarwater

Patrice M. Tate

Cynthia E. Tatum

Mary R. Taylor

June E. Tench

Johnny H. Thomas

Martha A. Thomas

Molly A. Thomas

Sallie J. Thomas

Judy M. Thompson

Sara A. Threlkeld

Nora G. Tiller

Charles R. Townsend

Geneva L. Trotter

Nancy L. Trotter

Sharon L. Trowell

Paula Tsiorbas

Peter Tsiorbas

Betsy Tucker

Dwight Turner

Jeffery Turner

Joann Turner

Ruth A. Turner

Charles E. Underwood

Hassie L. Underwood

Martha N. Underwood

Tonia K. Upshaw

Young S. Utash

Ruby L. Voyles

Stacy R. Waddell	William H. Whalen
Sang S. Walburg	Charles E. Whalen, Jr.
Marshall D. Wall	Linda Wheeler
James A. Wallace	Beatrice White
Debbie L. Waller	Mary F. Whitley
Nancy Waller	Katherine Whitmire
Broncile E. Warren	Margie N. Whitmire
Winnie B. Waters	Yvonne B. Whitmire
Edna S. Wehunt	Millie J. Whitworth
Patricia A. Wehunt	Bertie Wigington
Ronald B. Welborn	Rachel H. Wilbanks
Pamela L. Welch	Blondean Wilcox
Doris A. Whalen	Bessie J. Wiley
Jeffrey C. Whalen	Kelly A. Wiley

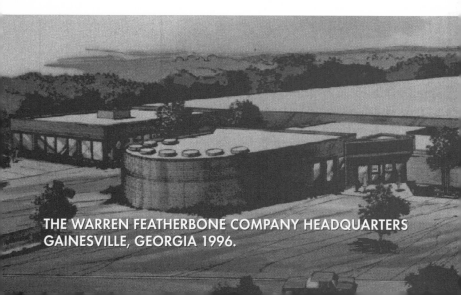

THE WARREN FEATHERBONE COMPANY HEADQUARTERS
GAINESVILLE, GEORGIA 1996.

Lavonia F. Wiley

Vernell Wiley

Mildred O. Wilkerson

Annie Williams

Frank R. Williams

Geneva C. Williams

Jennie L. Williams

Nancy L. Williams

Ophelia R. Williams

Pearlie M. Williams

Reba L. Williams

Tina Williams

Willene Williams

Diane L. Williamson

Sylvia L. Williamson

Doris V. Willis

Marion Willis

Shirley Wilson

Susan H. Wilson

Susan W. Wood

Tom R. Wood

Brenda Woosley

Geneva A. Worley

We're Optimistic!

cknowledgments

As proof of the significance of interdependence, this book represents the combined efforts of many people. Most of these people do not know each other, yet in this project they are all part of an orchestra that has produced this work. Whether they realize it or not, these are my coauthors, and I am very grateful to them.

Phil Bellury — *writer, researcher and thoughtful counselor*
Nell Whalen — *my wife, life partner and editor*

The following coauthors provided special encouragement and counsel:

Val Berryman and staff, *Michigan State University Museum*
Ken Breeden, *Georgia Dept. of Technical and Adult Education*
Phil Condit and Lee Lathrop, *The Boeing Company*
John Covington and Ed Hill, *Chesapeake Consulting*
Bernice Cramer, *Next Frame, Inc.*
J.W. Fanning, *retired vice president, University of Georgia*
Jim Frede, *Mercantile Stores*
Eli Goldratt, *The Goldratt Institute*

Rick Hamlin, *Guideposts Magazine*

Jan Hammond, *Harvard University School of Business*

Bill Holder, *Dillard's Department Stores*

Norm Johnsen, *J.C. Penney Company*

Susan Lord and Joe Berger, *Springs Industries*

Tom Leonard, *Samsonite*

John Lough, *University of Georgia*

Esther K. Martin, Three Oaks, Michigan

> *(Mrs. Martin worked for Warren Featherbone from 1933 to 1944 and has provided a firsthand account of that period)*

James Mathis, Sr., *retired, Trust Company Bank of North Georgia*

Roger Milliken, Tom Malone and Richard Dillard, *Milliken & Co.*

Eric Morgenthaler, *journalist*

Jack Tate and Linda Robertson, *Baby SuperStore*

Karen Schaffner, *Publisher, Apparel Industry Magazine*

Tom Wood, *The Warren Featherbone Company,* and his mother, Helen Wood *(Mrs. Wood is the daughter of H.H. Cutler)*

Finally, I want to thank my children, Eddie and Mary Ann, for their love and support. After reading the manuscript for this book, Mary Ann (age 20) exclaimed, "Dad, I think even my friends would read this!"

bout The Author

Charles E. "Gus" Whalen, Jr. is President and Chief Executive Officer of the Warren Featherbone Company of Gainesville, Georgia. In the tradition of the company, Gus Whalen is an innovator and pioneer in the apparel manufacturing industry. During his thirty years with Warren Featherbone, he has become a leader on the subject of industry partnerships and the interdependence of manufacturing in the United States.

In 1993, he established the Warren Featherbone Foundation to increase public awareness of the importance of U.S.-based manufacturing, with a special emphasis on educating youth about the career opportunities available in manufacturing.